Prayerbook for Catholics

Father Robert J. Fox, S.I.H.

CHRISTENDOM PUBLICATIONS
Route 3, Box 87
Front Royal, Virginia 22630

LC Cat. Classification No.: BX2130.F77
ISBN: 0-931888-08-5

NIHIL OBSTAT:
   Rev. Edward J. Berbusse, S.J., Censor Deputatis
   May 15, 1982

IMPRIMATUR:
   †Most Rev. Thomas J. Welsh
   Bishop of Arlington
   July 14, 1982

© Christendom Educational Corporation 1982

Publisher's Note: The publication of this book marks the foundation on September 13, 1982 of a new religious congregation, the Sons of the Immaculate Heart, in Redfield, South Dakota, under the leadership of the author, Fr. Robert Fox, and marks the S.I.H.'s first contribution to the cause of Christ.

Contents

About the Cover / 5
Introduction: On Prayer / 7
Part I: Four Purposes of Prayer / 10
Part II: The Trinity / 16
Part III: State of Life / 22
Part IV: The Sacraments / 34
Part V: The Church / 59
Part VI: The Last Things / 67
Part VII: Jesus, Savior / 73
Part VIII: Mary, Mother of God / 80
Part IX: Litanies / 94
Part X: The Rosary / 103
Part XI: Traditional Prayers Little Remembered / 109

The publication of this book was made possible in part through the support of the Christendom Publishing Group. Members are listed below:

Mr. Joseph C. Berzanskis
Mr. John F. Bradley
Mr. Joseph F. Brogan
Paul A. Busam, M.D.
Rev. Edward J. Connolly
Mr. John W. W. Cooper
The Dateno Family
Mr. Joseph L. DeStefano
Rev. Herman J. Deimel
Mr. Francis Donahue
Mr. Thomas J. Dowdall
Mr. John H. Duffy
Mrs. Clarence Ebert
Mr. J. P. Frank, Jr.
Mr. Richard L. Gerhards
Rev. Brian J. Hawker
Rev. John Horan
Mr. & Mrs. Andre Huck
Mrs. Doris L. Huff
Rev. Jeffrey A. Ingham
Mr. Herman Jadloski
Mr. Edward E. Judge
Mr. & Mrs. Albert Kais
Mr. William C. Koneazny
Miss Therese Lawrence
Rev. Harry J. Lewis

Very Rev. Victor O. Lorenz
Mr. George F. Manhardt
Mr. Thomas J. May
Mr. Joseph D. McDaid
Mr. & Mrs. Dennis P. McEneany
Mr. J. R. McMahon
Mr. Robert Cruise McManus
Rev. Edward J. Melvin, C.M.
Mr. Larry Miggins
Mr. James B. Mooney (St. Gerard Foundation)
Mr. Nicholas J. Mulhall
Mr. Joseph F. O'Brien
Mrs. Veronica M. Oravec
Mr. & Mrs. Joseph and Mary Peek
Mr. & Mrs. William H. Power, Jr.
Rev. T. A. Rattler, O.S.A.
Mrs. John F. Reid
Mr. Frank P. Scrivener
Dr. John B. Shea
Mrs. Mary Smerski
Mrs. Ann Spalding
Mr. Edward S. Szymanski
Rev. George T. Voiland
Mr. Fulton John Waterloo
Mrs. Mary Williams

This book is typeset in Garth Graphic Condensed and Bold Condensed type; text paper is 60 lb. Lakewood; paper cover is Kivar 3-17 (Firenze finish); cloth cover is Kivar 6 (Firenze finish).

About the Cover

The picture on the front cover, entitled "Reconciliation" was chosen by the author at a time in history when mankind is so in particular need of reconciliation, in need of calling upon the Divine Mercy. The original painting, by Anita Claus of Sioux Falls, South Dakota, has inspired young people to approach with trust the tribunal of mercy, the Confessional. We are inspired too by the encyclical of Pope John Paul II, **Dives in Misericordia** (Rich in Mercy). The Pope has said that from the beginning of his pontificate he has considered it his role to call men, the church and the world, to the Divine Mercy.

In his Encyclical, Pope John Paul wrote:

> . . . at no time, and in no historical period—especially at a moment as critical as our own—can the Church forget the prayer that is a cry for the mercy of God amid the many forms of evil which weigh upon humanity and threaten it. Precisely this is the fundamental right and duty of the Church in Christ Jesus, her right and duty towards God and towards humanity. The more the human conscience succumbs to secularization, loses its sense of the very meaning of the word 'mercy', moves away from God and distances itself from the mystery of mercy, the more the Church has the right and the duty to appeal to the God of mercy 'with loud cries' (cf. Hebrews 5:7). These 'loud cries' should be the mark of the Church of our times, cries uttered to God to implore His mercy, the certain manifestation of which she professes and proclaims as having already come in Jesus crucified and risen, that is, in the Paschal Mystery. It is this mystery which bears within itself the most complete revelation of mercy, that is, of that love which is more powerful than death, more

powerful than sin and every evil, the love which lifts man up when he falls into the abyss and frees him from the greatest threats.

May this prayerbook inspire its users with reverence for Merciful Love, which the Vicar of Jesus Christ on earth desires to be the mark of the Church in these times.

Fr. Fox

Introduction: On Prayer

Prayer is commonly defined as the lifting of the mind and heart to God. Praying is the response of our will in love to the awareness of the presence of God Who is all about us and within us.

God is everywhere. There are certain places where God dwells in a special way. This is true of heaven. It is true of the soul in grace. It is true of the sacramental presence of Jesus Christ in the Most Blessed Sacrament of the Altar. At times our response in love to the awareness of the presence of God may take in, in a special way, one or more of these modes of God's presence.

There are various kinds of prayer. The prayer of quiet is an internal peaceful repose by which the soul is captivated by the divine presence. The mind is thus enlightened by divine grace and spiritual delight permeates the entire person.

There is the prayer of simplicity whereby there is a simple loving thought of God, focusing on one or more of His attributes or some Christian mystery. Reasoning is put aside and in deep faith we lovingly rest under the operation of the Holy Spirit.

There is the prayer of union whereby the soul is conscious of a most intimate union with God and experiences His presence within the soul while the interior faculties are suspended. There is then an absence of distractions as the soul is wholly absorbed in God. There is great peace and joy in the soul and effort is not required as the soul ardently desires to glorify God and be detached from all created things while submissive to God's will and filled with love for neighbor as well.

Mental prayer is divided into three stages. First the 'purgative' way, according to the teaching of Sts. Teresa of Avila and John of the Cross. The soul's main concern at this stage is awareness of one's sins, sorrow for the past and the desire to make reparation for the offenses against God. The 'illuminative' way involves an enlightenment of the mind in the ways of God and a clear understanding of His will for one's state in life. Finally, the 'unitive' way involves a rather habitual awareness of God's presence and a disposition of conformity to the will of God. In reality, a person may shift back and forth among these three stages at any time while seeking growth in holiness.

The knowledge of our holy Catholic faith should form the basis of our prayer life. I look upon the dogmas of faith, the teachings of the one, holy Catholic and apostolic Church, as truths about the Person I love. That Person is Jesus Christ, the Word of God made flesh. Only through the God-Man, Mediator between heaven and earth, do we reach the Blessed Trinity.

Our perfect Model in prayer is Mary, the Mother of God and in Her Immaculate Heart I see the perfect Model of all that the Church is and hopes to become. As such, She is presented to us by Mother Church. In the cenacle, gathered with the Apostles who found it difficult to pray, even though taught by Jesus Christ Himself, was Mary, the Spouse of the Holy Spirit, from whom they learned to pray well. Thus in this prayerbook I turn often to Mary's Heart for inspiration in prayer.

St. Francis de Sales said that if, while saying vocal prayers, one's heart feels drawn to mental prayer, one ought not to resist it. I would suggest to the users of this prayerbook that if while using the choice of words I have provided, they find themselves uplifted to union with God, they should leave off from the printed word. Give room to the Holy Spirit.

St. John Vianney said that the more we pray, the more we desire to pray. The Psalmist said: "Taste and see that the Lord is sweet." St. Teresa of Avila said that there is only one way to find God, and that is by prayer. The perfect prayer is said to be the Lord's prayer for it involves all the elements of prayer, and yet the highest form of prayer is that of Jesus Christ offering Himself in Sacrifice upon the Cross which is perpetuated at Holy Mass. My own favorite prayers are the Mass and the Rosary. The prayers found in this small volume are simply an attempt to put to words some of the inspirations I've found while praying the Rosary, offering the Sacrifice of the Mass and reading meditatively the Word of God.

I cannot leave this introduction without a word on the holy Angels. They are too much ignored in our spiritual lives. And yet, God has given each one of us at least one of these holy creatures as a special Guardian who prays with us, adores with us, loves with us when we pray. Do not hesitate to call upon your holy Angel to pray with you.

Father Robert J. Fox
Sons of the Immaculate Heart
Redfield, South Dakota

Part I
FOUR PURPOSES OF PRAYER

Adoration

Thanksgiving

Petition

Reparation

Adoration

O Divine Majesty, God of heaven and earth, in You I live and move and have my being (Acts17:28). You are the Beginning and the End (Rv. 1:8). I came forth from You and You have destined me to spend eternity in Your eternal embrace.

If I climb the heavens, You are there. If I could fly to the point of sunrise, or westward across the seas, Your hand would still be guiding me, Your right hand holding me.

I fall down in adoration before You, O God, Who are everywhere. I am Your lowly creature and You are my Lord, my God, my all. I wish to annihilate myself before You as I am nothing. Still, You do not destroy anything You have made and all that You have made has been made in love.

By Your Divine will You have made me in love and destined me to share your Divine life of love. May I never offend You but fulfill the purpose of my existence, in which I shall find my happiness, by rendering glory to You, O God, the Source of all.

"My God, I believe, I adore, I trust and I love You. I beg pardon for those who do not believe, do not adore, do not trust and do not love You.

"O most holy Trinity, Father, Son and Holy Spirit, I adore You profoundly. I offer You the most precious Body, Blood, Soul and Divinity of Jesus Christ, present in all the tabernacles of the world, in reparation for the outrages, sacrileges and indifference by which He is offended. By the infinite merits of the Sacred Heart of Jesus, and the Immaculate Heart of Mary, I beg the conversion of poor sinners.

"My God, my God, I love You in the most Blessed Sacrament. Most holy Trinity, I adore You!"* Amen.

Thanksgiving

Heavenly Father, Creator of all, I offer You thanksgiving:
- for giving me natural life of body and soul;
  - for loving the world so much that You gave Your only begotten Son;
  - for giving me the gift of faith in Your Divine Son made man;
  - for having me baptized into the Mystical Body of Christ, the Church.

- for the food I have to eat and liquid I have to drink;
- for shelter and clothing to grant me comfort;
- for health of mind and body;
- for caring for me when I am ill;

- for promising me eternal life in heaven;
- for promising me the resurrection of the body if I eat the Body and drink the Blood of Your Son, Jesus Christ;
- for the gift of the Sacrament of penance so that I may be reconciled with You and my fellow man;
- for imprinting on my soul the Divine character of Christ in Baptism and Confirmation;
- for perpetuating the Sacrifice of Your Son's death on the

---

*From the prayers given to the Fatima children, approved by the Vatican.

Cross at every holy Mass.

I thank You heavenly Father, Son and Holy Spirit:

- for dwelling in my soul by sanctifying grace;
- for keeping me in existence at every moment of time;
- for seeking me out to lift me up when I fall;
- for granting me faith to believe in You and courage to trust You.
- for willing that I should come in love to the Father through Jesus Christ in the unity of the Holy Spirit;
- for granting me the graces I forget to request.

Amen.

Petition

My heavenly Father, I come to You in Jesus' name to request all that I need in mind, body, and spirit.

Grant me continued life that I may serve You and others.

Grant me continued faith that I may never deny You or Your Son Who became man and died on the Cross for me.

Grant me continuous grace that I may ever live sharing in Your Divine life.

Grant me health that I may perform the duties of my state in life.

Grant me peace with my family, relatives and friends.

Grant me wisdom to always do Your will and lead others to Your Son Incarnate in His holy Church.

Grant me trust in You my God that I may not trust in self.

Grant me the strength to live always according to the vocation in life You have given me and never to betray You or my fellow man.

Grant me the fulfillment of needs temporal or spiritual for which I am entirely dependent on You and for which I forget to ask.

Amen.

Reparation

Dear God of heaven and earth, of myself I am powerless to offer you satisfaction for my own past sins and those of the world. I offer myself but only as united to Jesus Christ. In Him, O heavenly Father, You are well pleased. I offer You the Body, Blood, Soul and Divinity of Jesus Christ present in our tabernacles and I unite myself to the Sacrifice of Your Son's Cross being perpetuated at Holy Mass throughout the world.

Look not upon my sins, but look upon the five precious wounds of Jesus Christ, now glorified in heaven, and see in Him the same Son made man constantly perpetuating His infinite act of love and reparation in the Sacrifice of the Mass. Gaze upon Your Son, the God-Man, our Brother, and accept His infinitely pleasing sacrifice in my name too, for I am one in Jesus Christ through faith, grace and the indelible seals of baptism and confirmation.

I offer You O heavenly Father, through the intercession of

Jesus Christ and the Immaculate Heart of Mary, all my prayers, works, joys and sufferings.

I am all Yours and all that I have is Yours, O most loving Jesus, through Mary Your Holy Mother.

"O my Jesus, forgive us our sins, save us from the fire of hell; lead all souls to heaven, especially those who are most in need of Your mercy."* Amen.

---

*From prayers given to the Fatima children, approved by the Vatican.

Part II
TRINITY

To the Glory of God the Father

Jesus Christ is Lord

To the Holy Spirit

To the Holy Trinity

Divine Mercy

To the Glory of God the Father

Heavenly Father, from all eternity You have existed, the uncreated Source of all. Your very nature is to exist. From You flows all that is and that has been made.

Before the billions of galaxies were created, You are. Before the countless angels were created to know and love You, You are. Before You created man in Your own image and likeness to know, love and serve You, You are. From all eternity You are infinitely happy and infinitely good. In time You shared Your Goodness and manifested it externally by creating the angels, the world and all that is in it, making man to govern in Your Name over Your creation.

You are Infinite Beauty, Infinite Goodness, Infinite Holiness, Infinite Power, Infinite Knowledge and Love, Infinite Happiness. Aside from You, O heavenly Father, I can find no happiness except in knowing and loving You. Therein I find holiness and goodness, for You alone are holy and You alone are good.

Glory to the Father, and to the Son, and to the Holy Spirit: as it was in the beginning, is now, and will be for ever. Amen.

Jesus Christ is Lord

Divine Lord and Master of our souls, although equal to God the Father, you emptied Yourself by being born in our likeness as men. You became a man in all things except sin.

You emptied Yourself, my loving Lord God and Savior, and

took the form of a slave, humbling Yourself, obediently accepting even death, death upon the Cross. Greater love than this no man has (Ph. 2:7-8, Jn. 15:13).

Because of Your infinite dignity and love the Father has highly exalted You and bestowed on You the name above every other name, so that at Your name, Lord Jesus, every knee must bend in the heavens, on the earth, and under the earth, and every tongue proclaim to the glory of God the Father: JESUS CHRIST IS LORD! (Ph. 2:9ff)

You are still the Lord of history. You control the reigns of time. While Satan seems to rule with sin, You have crushed His head, coming forth from the Woman overshadowed by the Holy Spirit (Gn. 3:15). Satan knows the time is limited in which he can roam the earth as a roaring lion seeking to devour men (1 Pt. 5:8) whose souls are made in the image and likeness of God, which the Evil One hates. While Satan has his hour, You Lord Jesus have Your day in which to rule and bring men to salvation when in faith and love we cry forth to the glory of God: JESUS CHRIST IS LORD!

Grant me that faith, that hope, that love, to proclaim to all by the words I speak, but even more by the actions of my life, by my service to You in fellow men, JESUS CHRIST IS LORD!
Amen.

To the Holy Spirit

Spirit of Love, breath of the Father, sent forth from the Father and the Son to fill the world with the fire of love, come into our hearts. Live in us as in a temple, vivifying, sanctifying, making us ever more into the Image of Jesus Christ.

You dwell in souls in the state of grace as in a temple. You are the soul of the Church and keep it in the truth. You are the spirit of unity and bind all men who are open to the living water of grace into one Mystical Body of Christ.

Give us new hearts and place a new spirit within us, taking from our bodies stony hearts and giving us natural hearts alive with God. Permit each one of us to speak the many languages of faith and love to all the world.

O Holy Spirit, may I be open to Your love and Person, living, breathing within me, as in a temple. May I never allow the waters of Divine life within me to become lifeless, stagnant, dead by not sharing the gifts and fruits of the Holy Spirit. Rather, may I have life and have it more abundantly.

Sweet Guest of my soul, sanctify me more and more. Amen.

To the Holy Trinity*

O Most Holy Trinity, I adore You who are dwelling by your Grace within my soul.

O most Holy Trinity, who are dwelling by Your grace within my soul, make me love You more and more.

---

*From the **Enchiridion of Indulgences**, 1968.

O Most Holy Trinity, who are dwelling by Your grace within my soul, sanctify me more and more.

Abide with me, O lord; be my true joy.

Amen.

Divine Mercy

Eternal Father, pleading for the Divine mercy for myself and for all of humanity, I offer You the Body, Blood, Soul and Divinity of Your beloved Son, Our Lord Jesus Christ, in atonement for my sins and those of the entire world.

Holy, Mighty and Immortal God, have mercy on me and on the entire world. Because of the sorrowful passion and death of Jesus Christ have mercy and grant us that peace which the world cannot give (Jn. 14:27).

Lord Jesus, I place my trust in You. My loving and merciful Lord Jesus Christ, by the blood and water which gushed forth from Your side when Your Heart was opened by a lance on the Cross, wash away all our sins and grant Your Divine life of grace to souls.

I offer You, heavenly Father, the loud cries and tears which Your Son Jesus Christ offered to You when He was in the flesh upon earth (Heb. 5:7). O God, Who are Providence, Who are inscrutable Mystery, the Mystery of Love and Truth, of Truth and Love, hear Your holy Church in Its ceaseless praise of You and Its intercession for the salvation of the entire world, as thousands of priests, religious and laity about the world pray the Divine Office daily.* Let our loud cries for mercy in unity with Your Son be the mark of the Church of our times, times which are lost in so many forms of evil and sin.

O Holy Spirit, enkindle in us the fire of Divine love, sanctify us more and more. O merciful Love, as we cry to You, may it be true of our times, "because of the Lord's great mercy we are not consumed" (Lam. 3:22). Amen.

---

*Now called **Christian Prayer: The Liturgy of the Hours**, available in inexpensive editions, and recommended for use by the laity as well as by priests and religious.

Part III
STATE OF LIFE

Single

Courtship

Single Parents

Parents

Marriage

Religious

Priests

Seminarians

Papacy

Bishops

Unborn Human Life

A Child Fallen Away

Single

Lord Jesus, may my vocation to the single life prove fruitful in serving others and coming closer to God the Father through You in the unity of the Holy Spirit. You have not called me to Matrimony, and so I desire to live in close intimacy with you alone, my Lord and my God.

I am never alone. The Most Blessed Trinity dwells in my soul by grace. My Guardian Angel is ever at my side. Assist me, my Lord, in seeing Jesus Christ in all whom I meet.

Mary, you are my Queen and my Mother. I cherish you, ever-Virgin Mother of God. The sweetness of your Immaculate Heart is sufficient to answer the needs of my heart for warmth and affection as you lead me to intimacy with the Blessed Trinity. Keep me ever pure in the embrace of the Divine Love. Amen.

Courtship

O Most Holy Trinity, Three in One, I come to the Divine Family which is God, Father Son and Holy Spirit, and beg your Divine guidance in the choice of a spouse. I believe that my vocation in life is Holy Matrimony. Assist me in keeping my courtship pure and holy for I am convinced that a courtship of sin can never lead to a successful, holy marriage.

My courtship is based on selfishness if in any way I lead my partner into sin. Selfishness is never true love. May I rather be an instrument of You my loving Lord, in leading my partner to goodness and holiness.

St. Joseph, virginal Father of Jesus Christ and husband of Mary, I beg your powerful intercession in keeping my courtship pure and holy and ask that you assist me in the choice of a spouse according to the Divine will.

Mother Mary, ever-Virginal Mother of God and Spouse of the Holy Spirit, lead me and my special friend to goodness and holiness all the days of our lives. Amen.

Single Parents

Dear Lord of heaven and earth, it is not easy living alone with the children You have given me and apart from the one to whom you lawfully united me in Holy Matrimony. However difficult, I accept Your Divine Will which has permitted our separation by _____ (name the circumstances).

I beg for strength, for courage to represent You my Lord to my children, those under my care. Keep me pure and consistent in loving authority over my children. Keep me ever close to Your Divine Heart, O Jesus.

Mother Mary, I fly to the refuge of your Immaculate Heart and consecrate myself and all in my care to you.

Without You, O Lord, I can do nothing. But in You my Lord Jesus, Who strengthen me, I can do all things. Amen.

Parents

Heavenly Father, keep our family always one in Jesus Christ. You have granted us the great privilege and dignity of sharing in Your power of creation, indeed in the crown of your creation, through children made to your own image and likeness. We thank You for each child You have given us. We pray to be worthy of this great honor and that we may be your instruments as the primary educators of our children in the fullness of true Faith, and that our example may provide them the formation they need to become firm in the practice of our Holy Catholic Faith. We consecrate ourselves and each one of our children to the Holy Family of Jesus, Mary and Joseph.

Protect each one of our children, O heavenly Father. May the Holy Spirit always dwell in them as in a temple. May our family as a miniature Mystical Body of Christ always reflect the reality of the universal Church. Guide each one of our children in the choice of his vocation and in perseverance therein. Give them health, sufficient means of support and above all eternal life. We pray for (name each child) and especially for (name) who at this time is in special need. Amen.

Marriage

O Lord grant us a holy marriage. May we always realize that Matrimony is a sacrament binding until death and "what God has joined together, let no man put asunder" (Mt. 19:6).

As a (husband/wife) I have the duty of not only working for my own salvation but also assisting my spouse and any children God may give us in becoming saints.

Lord God, the inspired Word of God informs us that the family is a miniature Mystical Body of Jesus Christ (see especially **Ephesians**). Each family united in Christ is an image of the universal Church. God has promised in virtue of the Sacrament of Matrimony all the graces needed to be a successful (husband/wife) and (father/mother). Lord Jesus, may we never reject Your graces which lead us to happiness and perfection in human love upon earth and to Divine love in heaven.

May our marriage prove to be both love-giving and life-giving. May we never separate our love of each other from the natural power of life. May we manifest our true love for each other and for God by self-control, sacrifice, patience, kindness, understanding, and forgiveness and may the practice of the Christian virtues in pure love lead to peace with God and each other and with each member of our family.

May we as parents be the first teachers and formers in the Faith of those children God desires us to bring into this world, destined for heaven. May we keep in mind that some day each one of our children will in turn answer a call from God. May they be instruments to pass on the true Faith to future generations because we taught it fully now and lived it in loving example. Amen.

Religious

Lord Jesus, whatever your religious do under vows is more meritorious than what others do with no vow. Your special chosen ones, pledged to poverty, chastity and obedience, by their vows add the virtue of religion to the merit of their holy actions. May the vows of Your religious give firmness and constancy to their wills, render them more perfectly in conformity with Your Divine Will, and perfect the work which they accomplish.

May Your religious sacrifice themselves for the love of You, O God, as they sacrifice their free will unto union with the Divine Will. May your religious always be mindful that the state of virginity or of celibacy is preferable to marriage and is a higher calling from God.

May Your religious, given greater freedom from earthly cares, manifest to all the faithful the heavenly goods which will one day be possessed by all the Blessed in heaven when we have all arrived at our true home.

May all religious spread throughout the whole world the good news of Christ by the integrity of their faith, their love for God and neighbor, their devotion to the Cross, and their hope of future glory. May their witness be seen by all, and may our Father in heaven be glorified. Thus, too, with the prayerful aid of you, O most loving Virgin Mary, God's Mother, whose life is a rule of life for all, may religious communities experience a daily growth in numbers, and yield a richer harvest of fruits that bring salvation. Amen.

Priests

Lord Jesus, each one of Your priests bears upon his ordained soul the indelible mark of your holy priesthood, the Divine character of Christ the Priest for all eternity. Each one of them has the power to act in Your very Person in consecrating bread and wine into Your Body, Blood, Soul and Divinity and so to re-enact the sacrificial death of You, dear Jesus, which redeemed the world and gave the heavenly Father perfect adoration and reparation.

Grant to all men the grace to respect priests as other Christs. Grant to priests the grace to always remember their dignity while remaining Your humble servants, Lord.

Keep them from loneliness, for they have You, O Lord. Keep them pure, for their bodies are totally Yours. Keep them spotless as the host, as white as lilies, and may no one ever say of them that they are just like other men. They are rather men set apart for Divine service, for perpetuating the Sacrifice of the Cross, for consecrating the world into Your very self, O Lord. Never let them forget that they have Your power to forgive sins, and are commissioned to preach the Word of God Incarnate.

O heavenly Mother Mary, you can gaze upon the priests of your Church and call them in a unique way Sons of your Immaculate Heart. We beg you to take special care of these special sons. Amen.

Seminarians

Lord Jesus, You said to Your Apostles, "You have not chosen me. I have chosen you" (Jn. 15:16). Give increased faith, hope, love and purity to our seminarians. Keep them for yourself, dear Lord. They are Yours and Yours they wish to be.

O Mary, Mother of the Church, your holy will was involved in giving the world the High Priest, your Son, Jesus Christ. God sent the angel Gabriel to you and it was your choice to accept the Divine motherhood so that the Word might be made flesh and dwell among us as Priest-Mediator. Priests are other-Christs and your will today is involved in the call of every young man to follow in the footsteps of your Son as one of His priests.

Protect our seminarians and keep them under your motherly mantle. You have called them to be sons of your Immaculate Heart. In living prayerful lives of faith and love, in studying the Word of God, with you as Mother and Model, they will be formed more and more into the likeness of your loving Son, Jesus Christ.

Obtain for them courage and perseverance in their studies and assist them to overcome the temptations that call them back to the world. Assist them in tasting to see how sweet the Lord is and to realize that, joined in chastity to Jesus Christ, they will receive a hundredfold already upon this earth as they become one day fathers in Christ to the many children of your holy Church. And then, once having given the gift of themselves to Jesus Christ in the refuge of your Immaculate Heart, protect them so that never will they take back this gift from your Son, the eternal High Priest. Amen.

Papacy

Divine and loving Jesus, I believe that the Pope is the visible head of Your Church upon earth as You are the invisible Head of the Mystical Body.

Lord Jesus, You said to Peter the first Pope, "You are 'Rock', and on this rock I will build my church" (Mt. 16:18). You promised that the gates of hell shall never prevail against Your Church with Peter the Rock as chief visible teacher who would receive the special gift of the Holy Spirit to keep the Church one and in the truth.

Send forth from Yourself and the Father, O Jesus Christ, the Holy Spirit Who is the Soul of the Church, to give our pope that strength he needs in facing a world which often desires to turn its back on the Word of God. Give to the bishops of the world the wisdom, strength and humility to remain always one with the Holy Father, the pope, in the teaching of faith and morals. Grant to the faithful the abiding joy they can know only by living in loyalty to the true teachings of Holy Mother Church under the authority of Peter which is vested in Pope John Paul II (or subsequent pope). Amen.

Bishops

Lord Jesus, keep the bishops of Your holy Church united under the supreme authority of our Holy Father, the Pope. He is the chief shepherd and our Lord desires that there be but "one flock and one shepherd" (Jn. 10:16). The Word of God says the Church consists of "one Lord, one faith and one baptism" (Eph. 4:5).

Grant our Bishops, Lord Jesus, the courage in the Holy Spirit and trust in the Lord to boldly proclaim the truths of the one, holy Catholic and apostolic Faith without compromise. Grant them the reward that is theirs as teachers of the holy Faith so that they may shine for all eternity as bright stars in heaven unto the glory of the Blessed Trinity. Amen.

Unborn Human Life

O Almighty God, Creator of heaven and earth and all things, you create today millions of human beings who are never permitted to see the light of day because of the sin of abortion. Grant to mankind the wisdom to respect human life at every stage of development. You infuse souls into innocent babies even while still in their mothers' wombs, their temporary homes. Grant that no one deprive your most innocent ones the privilege of holy baptism whereby they may be born again to Your supernatural life by grace.

One soul in Your eyes, Almighty God, is of more value than the whole created universe. Accept the precious blood of Your Son Jesus Christ present on our altars and in our tabernacles throughout the world in reparation for the sins of abortive murder.

Even before Your Divine Son was born of Mary, dear God,

when Your holy Mother greeted Elizabeth shortly after the conception of the Divine Child, Elizabeth asked, "How am I worthy that the Mother of my Lord should come to me?" Long before the birth of the Divine Child, the Holy Spirit inspired Elizabeth to call Mary "Mother" and the unborn Child, her "Lord."

Almighty God, remove the scourge of abortion from the face of the earth. Amen.

Child Fallen Away

Dear God, I come to You with a heart of sorrow over love for my child who has drifted from the practice of the holy Catholic faith. Look upon this (son/daughter) of mine with Your loving and forgiving mercy. Bring this child back into the embrace of Holy Mother Church that soon (he/she) may receive once again forgiveness in Your Sacrament of Penance and be nourished with Your Body, Blood, Soul and Divinity in Holy Communion.

O Saint _____ (name saint), patron saint of my child, intercede in heaven for (his/her) salvation. Angel Guardian of my child, you who were appointed to the charge of (his/her) soul, intercede constantly before the heavenly throne of the Most Holy Trinity. Beg of Mary, the Queen of Angels to send forth all the Angels of God along with yourself, O Holy Angel, to inspire my child to return to the path of salvation I once attempted to teach (him/her). I beg my own Guardian Angel to go to my child to inspire (him/her) to return.

Give me the strength to bear this cross, and I offer to You, O Sacred Heart of Jesus and Immaculate Heart of Mary, the pain that I feel, so that some day my child will return and I may glorify God forever in heaven with this child whom I love. Amen.

Part IV
SACRAMENTS

Baptism: Renewal of Vows

Confirmation

Confession

Manner of Going to Confession

Prayer Before Confession

Instruction of John Paul II

Examination of Conscience

Prayer After Confession

Holy Eucharist: Blessed Sacrament

Devotions Before Holy Communion

Devotions After Holy Communion

Anima Christi

Baptism: Renewal of Vows

God the Father, I believe in You as Creator of heaven and earth.

I believe that You, Jesus Christ, are His only Son, who were born of the Virgin Mary, crucified, died and were buried and who rose from the dead and are now seated at the right hand of the Father.

I believe in the Holy Spirit, the Holy Catholic Church, the communion of saints, the forgiveness of sins, the resurrection of the body, and life everlasting.

God the Father of my Lord Jesus Christ, I believe that through baptism You freed me from sin, gave me new birth by water and the Holy Spirit and received me into Your holy people (Jn. 3:5). I believe that just as Christ was annointed Priest, Prophet and King so I was engrafted into His Mystical Body, the Church, and share in His Divine privileges unto everlasting life.

In renewal of my baptismal vows:

I reject sin, so as to live in the freedom of God's children.

I reject the glamor of evil, and refuse to be mastered by sin.

I reject Satan, father of sin and prince of darkness.

Assist me, O Holy Trinity, in remaining true to these promises. Amen.

Confirmation

All powerful God, Father of our Lord Jesus Christ, by water and the Holy Spirit you freed me from sin and gave me new life.

When I received the Sacrament of Confirmation You sent your Holy Spirit upon me to be my Helper and Guide. I call upon the graces of Confirmation which sealed me eternally with a special indelible mark of Jesus Christ so that the Holy Spirit will re-enkindle in me the spirit of wisdom and understanding, the spirit of right judgment and courage, the spirit of knowledge and reverence.

Fill me with the spirit of wonder and awe at Your Presence, Almighty God. Assist me as a witness to my faith in Jesus Christ to all about me. I ask this through Jesus Christ my Lord. Amen.

Confession

O Jesus, I believe that when I confess my sins to a duly authorized and ordained priest, it is the same as confessing my sins to You, for You have shared Your priestly powers with Your priests. When I receive the absolution of Your priest, my Lord, it is really You who wash away my sins in Your most precious blood.

You said to Your Apostles: "As the Father has sent me, so I send you." Then You breathed on them and said: "Receive the Holy Spirit. If you forgive men's sins, they are forgiven them;

if you hold them bound, they are held bound" (Jn. 20:21-23).

Lord, I have a certain sign from You my God that my sins are forgiven, when, with a firm intention of working to avoid sin in the future, and with sorrow for my sins which have wounded You, I approach your priesthood as found in men, and confess sincerely and completely according to a correctly formed conscience, and promise to do penance for my sins.

When I hear the words of Your priests, "I absolve You from your sins . . .", I then know that my soul is purified through Your most precious blood and I live, sharing the life of God in my soul, with the most Blessed Trinity dwelling within me as in a temple.

May I never fear this holy sacrament but rather receive what You intended it to be, a sacrament of mercy and peace. Thank You dear Lord for this Sacrament of Reconciliation. Amen.

Manner of Going to Confession

Priest opens confessional door:

Priest: May the peace of Christ Jesus be with you.

Priest and Penitent: In the name of the Father, and of the Son, and of the Holy Spirit. Amen. (While making the sign of the Cross.)

Priest: May God, Who has enlightened every heart, help you to know your sins and trust in His mercy.

Penitent: Amen.

Father may read a scriptural quotation, and then you may make your confession. If the priest does not give the greeting above, begin immediately with what follows as the priest opens the door.

Penitent: Father, my last confession was _____ ago. I am a _____ (state of life). These are my sins: (Give number and circumstances which change the nature of the sins.) I am sorry for these and all the sins of my past life and those which I cannot now remember. I humbly ask pardon of God and penance and absolution of you, Father.

The priest then talks to the penitent and gives a penance, and asks the penitent to recite a good act of contrition, waiting while the penitent recites an act of contrition in his own words or according to a traditional form, e.g., "Oh my God, I am heartily sorry for having offended You", etc.

Priest: (Now gives absolution) God, the Father of Mercies, through the death and resurrection of His Son has reconciled the world to Himself and sent the Holy Spirit among us for the forgiveness of sins: through the ministry of the Church may God give you pardon and peace, and **I absolve you from your sins in the name of the Father, and of the Son, and of the Holy Spirit.**
Penitent: Amen.
Priest: Give thanks to the Lord, for He is good.
Penitent: His mercy endures forever.
Priest: The Lord has freed you from your sins. Go in peace.
Penitent: Thank you, Father.

The penitent now reenters the main body of the Church for penance and thanksgiving.

Prayer Before Confession

O my Father, Divine Mercy, I come to You in and through the grace of repentance so as to receive forgiveness by having my sins washed away in the most precious Blood of my Lord, Jesus Christ.

O heavenly Father, look upon the passion, crucifixion and death of Your Divine Son become Man, my Lord and my Savior, as He merited my redemption. Gaze upon His five most precious wounds before the heavenly throne. It was these wounds from which poured His precious Blood out of mercy for poor lost sinners, including myself. I thank You, Jesus, for suffering and dying on the Cross for me and the whole world.

Holy Spirit, help me to know my sins and to be sorry for them. Grant me the grace of a firm purpose of amendment, the intention to avoid sin and the occasions of sin in the future. Help me to confess my sins humbly, sincerely and completely to Your representative the priest, with whom You have shared Your powers as High Priest unto the forgiveness of sin. I desire to perform whatever penance Your priest gives me to make reparation for my sins.

I am sorry for my sins, O Divine Lord Jesus Christ, as I call upon Your merciful Love, offering to the Eternal Father Your Body, Blood, Soul and Divinity in atonement for my sins and those of the whole world. Amen.

Instruction of Pope John Paul II

"At the sight of the Lord the disciples rejoiced. 'Peace be with you,' he said again. 'As the Father has sent me, so I send you.' Then he breathed on them and said: 'Receive the Holy Spirit. If you forgive men's sins, they are forgiven them; if you hold them bound, they are held bound'" (Jn. 21:20-23).

Pope John Paul II spoke as follows to priests regarding the need for Confession:

> In this context of consoling Eucharistic fervor which leads innumerable faithful, particularly the young, to approach the Divine Banquet, you will also not tire to enlighten consciences about the due dispositions with which they must receive Holy Communion. Dignity, purity, and innocence are the main gifts recommended by St. Paul to the early communities of Corinth: "Whoever, therefore, eats the Bread or drinks the cup of the Lord in an unworthy manner will be guilty of profaning the Body and Blood of the Lord. Let a man examine himself, and so eat of the Bread and drink of the cup. For anyone who eats and drinks without discerning the Body eats and drinks judgement upon himself" (1 Cor. 11:27-29). A sacramental catechesis, planned as it should be, cannot neglect such an important task. As you well know, the theory according to which the Eucharist forgives mortal sin without the sinner having recourse to the sacrament of Penance, is **not** reconcilable with the teaching of the Church. It is true that the Sacrifice of the Mass, from which all grace comes to the Church, obtains for the sinner the gift of conversion, without which forgiveness is not possible, but that does not mean that those who have committed a mortal sin can approach Eucharistic communion without having first become reconciled with God by means of the priestly

ministry.

The sacrament of Penance is the ordinary and necessary way for all those who, after Baptism, have fallen into serious sin. Its scope is not limited however, just to wiping out sins in hearts that have repented, but it is also the manifestation of the merciful goodness of God and of His glory according to the triple expression of the great Bishop of Hippo: confession of life, confession of faith, confession of praise (**confessio vitae, confessio fidei, confessio laudis**). With this sacrament, as the rite of Penance says in n. 7, "The Church proclaims her faith, gives thanks to God for the freedom with which Christ freed us, offers her life as a spiritual sacrifice in praise of the glory of God." It must not be forgotten, therefore, that the celebration of Penance is always an act of worship in which the Church praises the holiness of God and 'confesses' the marvels of His merciful love, which heals, raises from the dead and sacrifices.

Examination of Conscience

Before receiving the Sacrament of Penance (Confession) each one should ask himself questions such as those suggested here:

Penance:
1) Have I had the proper attitude toward this sacrament, realizing that it is a special gift of God's love and mercy, not simply

a burden, as revealed in Scripture? (John 20:23). Do I look upon this Sacrament as a personal encounter with Jesus Christ so as to be set free from sin, to begin a new and deeper life of grace in friendship with Almighty God? Have I stayed away from availing myself of God's gift of mercy for a long time? 2) Have I deliberately concealed mortal sins in past confessions? (If so, go back to your last good confession, sharing this with the priest and confess all serious sins.) 3) Did I perform the penance given me in my last confession conscientiously? 4) If guilty of mortal sin, did I go to Confession before receiving Holy Communion? 5) Have I sought a priest-confessor who will best help me live the true teaching of Jesus and His Church?

Reparation:

1) Have I been concerned about making satisfaction only for my own past sins? 2) Do I ever offer sacrifices, Masses, Holy Communions, good works in reparation for the sins in the world? 3) Do I look upon each Friday as a day for special penance? 4) (During Lent) Did I intensify the spirit of penance and reparation? Did I fast and abstain on the days appointed?

God's Word: Teachings of the Church:

1) Do I really seek to know the truths of my Catholic faith? 2) Have I read and studied **reliable** Catholic sources and listened to the pronouncements of the Pope? 3) Have I rather listened to those who dissent from the official Church to justify my weak will and bad intentions? 4) Have I given scandal to others by criticizing the teachings of the Church? 5) Have I listened attentively to instructions on the faith? 6) Have I strongly defended and professed the Catholic faith? 7) Have I covered

up my faith in private or public life rather than let my Catholic faith be manifest?

Prayer:
1. Have I begun and ended each day with prayer? 2) Do I pray with my mind and heart or only with mechanical words? 3) Have I prayed in time of temptation? 4) Have I turned my thoughts to God occasionally during the day? 5) Have I offered my joys, sorrows, works to God in prayerful reparation? 6) Have I spent any time in prayer before my Divine Lord Jesus Christ in the Most Blessed Sacrament of the tabernacle?

Language:
1. Have I misused the Name of God? 2) Have I been guilty of blasphemy, swearing falsely? 3) Have I used disrespectful language to shock, show irreverence? Have I shown by my language any disrespect for God's Mother, the Angels and Saints? 4) Have I given scandal by my words, actions?

Lord's Day, Holy Days
1) Have I recognized that it is mortally sinful deliberately not to participate in the Sacrifice of the Mass on Sundays and Holy Days of obligation? 2) Have I done shopping and other unnecessary work on Sundays? 3) Have I used the entire Lord's Day for rest or recreation, in a special spiritual frame of mind?

Materialism:
1) Do I have other gods than the one true God whom I worship by being attached to money, property, superstition, spiritism, or occult practices? 2) Am I generous in sharing my abundance or with those in need or do I selfishly wish to build up large

material security rather than trust in Divine Providence? Do I think I must frequently have new and better things? 3) Was I selfish and did I not contribute to the support of the Church and apostolic works of charity? 4) Am I concerned about the poor and underprivileged in a practical way, giving help where I can? 5) Do I envy material possessions others have, unsatisfied with what God has provided for me? 6) Am I poor in spirit?

Mass and the Sacraments:

1) Have I participated in the Sacrifice of the Mass with a spirit of faith, love and adoration? 2) While at holy Mass, have I remembered that the Sacrifice of the Cross is being perpetuated? 3) Did I offer at Mass all I am and do and have in union with the Father? 4) Did I arrive on time, stay until the Mass was completed? 5) Did I work spiritually to appreciate unity in Christ with the other members of the parish by active participation? 6) Was my spirit at Holy Mass to give adoration or only to get something from God? 7) Was I in the state of sanctifying grace when I received Holy Communion, realizing it would be a mortal sin of sacrilege otherwise? 8) Did I prepare well to receive our Eucharistic Lord and make a thanksgiving? 9) Did my spirit of thanksgiving extend even after the Mass was completed? 10) Did I show proper reverence and adoration for the Real Presence of Jesus Christ in the most Blessed Sacrament of the tabernacle? 11) Am I warm and friendly to fellow parishioners before and after Holy Mass, without visiting with others before our Eucharistic Lord? 12) Have I made an effort to make visitors and new parishioners feel welcome in my parish family?

Charity:

1) Have I had a genuine love for others or borne hatred in my heart for anyone? 2) Have I shown concern for others or simply used them for my own ends? 3) Have I done unto others what I would not want done unto myself? 4) Have I lied? Have I been guilty of calumny or detractions in talking about others, thus ruining their reputations? If so, have I made an effort to repair the harm done to another's good name? 5) Have I made efforts to love even those opposed to me? 6) Have I loved God for Himself above all things, truly putting God first? 7) Have I looked down on others less fortunate than myself or on those of a different culture, color or race? 8) Have I prayed for the suffering souls in Purgatory? 9) Have I developed a love for God's Mother Mary, St. Joseph, the Angels and Saints? 10) Do I ever pray for priestly and religious vocations? Do I pray for the Pope, my bishop, my local pastor? 11) Do I pray for the welfare and unity of the universal Church?

Purity:

1) Have I made efforts to be truly pure of heart, realizing the body is destined for resurrection? 2) Have I avoided television, movies, and publications that downgrade the virtue of holy purity? 3) Have I been modest in dress or immodest so as to appeal to the sensuality of others? 4) Have I dressed conscious that the body should be a temple of the Holy Spirit? 5) Have I listened to or told stories that lower moral standards or conduct in others? 6) Have I been prompt in banishing impure thoughts and desires? 7) Did I date a person whom I knew I could never marry because of divorce? 8) Did I date a person

whom I knew was a serious occasion of sin to me? 9) Have I been guilty of impure acts alone (masturbation) or with others (adultery, fornication), which acts are serious offenses which must be avoided? 10) Have I honestly confessed my sins against purity as to number and circumstances, or vaguely so as to disguise the seriousness of my guilt? 11) Have I sought help from a confessor who would help direct me to a life of purity? 12) Did I pray when tempted against purity? 13) Have I avoided the sacraments which could help me live a life of purity? 14) Have I been guilty of leading another into impurity by word or deed? 15) Have I let down my guard against impurity by drinking to excess? 16) Have I failed to strengthen my will by acts of penance and self-denial? 17) Have I controlled my eyes? 18) Have I recognized that (for the unmarried) passionate embracing or touching is seriously sinful? 19) If married, have I enticed or shown affection which is due only to my spouse? 20) Do I have a contraceptive mentality or do I practice unnatural or artificial birth control which is condemned by God and His Church?

Justice:

1) Have I made restitution for taking things not rightfully mine? 2) Have I given an honest day's work for an honest day's pay? 3) Have I shared my possessions with the less fortunate? 4) Have I worked for justice to the oppressed, the misfortunate and have I helped those in poverty to better their condition? 5) Have I given needed help to the elderly, the infirm? 6) Was I just to those who work under me or over me? 7) Did I demand my rights without consideration for the rights of others? 8) Did I

run my business according to honest Christian principles or do I think the end justifies the means? 9) Did I respect the property of others? 10) Did I speak up and act for the right to life for the unborn? 11) Did I realize that in justice I owe God worship on His day and the living of a Christian life throughout the week? 12. Do I realize that justice requires support of the church according to my honest means, locally as well as on the diocesan, national and world-wide levels?

Respect for Authority:
1) Have I obeyed all lawful authority, civil and religious? 2) Have I, by attitude and deed, respected the dignity and authority of Christ's chief Vicar on earth, the Pope? 3) Have I turned the conversation to a positive and correct approach when in the presence of others whose attitude toward Church authority and teachings has been wrong? 4) Have I respected authority by using it justly and in charity when I had a responsibility myself to exercise it? Or have I neglected to use my authority when there was real need, thus eventually causing harm to others? 5) Have I lacked humility, been guilty of pride, in not accepting lawful authority?

Family Life:
1) Have I contributed to happiness and harmony in my family by patience, kindness, forgiveness and understanding? 2) Have I obeyed my parents? 3) Have I taken a united front with my spouse in disciplining children in justice and love? 4) Have I participated in daily family prayer? 5) Have I helped instruct children in the faith or delegated it entirely to others, forgetting that parents are the primary educators of their children? 6) Did

I give good example to my children by participating in Holy Mass and frequenting the sacraments? 7) Do I take an active interest in whether each of my children is growing in knowledge and love of his faith and identifying with Christ's Church? Do I observe whether my teenagers go to confession frequently? 8) Do I really know each one of my children? 9) Have I been a good example in manifesting positive Catholic thinking and conversations and by exercising loving authority as a parent? 10) Have I been sensitive to the needs of my spouse? 11) Have I used family income for proper support or wasted money and given scandal by excessive drink, gambling? 12) Have I caused hurt to self and family members by the use of drugs or drink? 13) Am I a loving family member? 14) Have I prudently guided my older children into Catholic marriages or advised them kindly to select a spouse who will help lead them to salvation? 15) Have I been faithful to my (husband/wife) in my heart and in relations with others? 16) Do I visit and keep in frequent touch with elderly parents? 17) Have I given sufficient time to each of my children or am I more married to my work? 18) Do I provide good Catholic reading in my home and watch what literature comes into the home? 19) As a parent do I have good moral standards as to which television programs are harmful and which can assist to develop wholesome Christian principles in family members? 20) Do I understand love for family members means sacrificing self? 21) Have I tried to uplift my spouse in moments of suffering, discouragement? 22) Do I show appreciation for my spouse's (parent's) good points or only criticize negatively? 23) Have I caused pain and sorrow to my parents?

Apostolic Christianity:
1) Have I engaged in apostolic and charitable work of the Church and of my local parish? 2) Do I look to the Church only to receive and not to give? 3) Have I had a spirit of evangelization to share the true faith with others locally, and beyond my parish for the foreign missions? 4) Have I tried to instruct the ignorant so as to understand the Church properly? 5) Have I criticized the church while making no positive contributions? 6) Do I realize that I too am the Church and have obligations to witness for Christ by using the grace of Confirmation? 7) Have I been a support to the bishop, priests and religious? 8) Have I been a cause of disunity in the parish by word or deed? 9) Do I pray for fallen aways? 10) Do I pray for and help if possible or only criticize those who have given scandal? 11) Have I been honest and open with my confessor so as to grow in holiness? 12) Do I look to the Sacrifice of the Mass and Holy Communion as chief forms of growing in charity and the spirit of unity with other members of the Mystical Body of Christ, the Church? Do I thereby approach the Holy Eucharist reconciled to God and fellow human beings? 13) Do I perform my duties as a citizen? 14) Do I work to grow in knowledge of God by solid spiritual reading? 15) Do I use the talents God has given me to serve Him and my fellow man?

Prayer After Confession

Thank You Lord Jesus for forgiving me my sins in Your Merciful Love through the absolution of Your priest. I am not worthy of the great mercy You have bestowed upon me so often in the past and at present.

I rejoice at being in the state of sanctifying grace. Now I know with the certainty of faith because of Your Divine promises that I share in the life of God, and that the Most Blessed Trinity dwells within my soul as a temple. Trusting in Your love and mercy I believe You have forgiven my sins and I thank You Lord Jesus for having died on the Cross, for love of me and all souls, so that we could have our sins forgiven and spend eternity with You in heaven.

I desire always to remain in Your grace. Help me never to offend You in the future. Amen.

Holy Eucharist: Sacrifice of the Mass

O Divine and loving Jesus Christ, my Lord and my God, You who once became obedient unto death, even unto death on the Cross, I believe that every holy Mass perpetuates the infinite Sacrifice of the Cross which wrought salvation for the whole world unto the glory of the heavenly Father.

As often as we eat the body and drink the chalice of the Lord, we show forth Your death, O Jesus Christ, until You come. I believe that to be present at the Sacrifice of the Mass is essentially the same as being present at the Sacrifice once offered physically on the Cross on Good Friday afternoon. Only the manner of offering differs. I believe that the self-same Sacrifice is perpetuated.

O Jesus, the heavenly Father, looking down upon holy Mass being offered today, sees You His Son Jesus Christ re-enacting the Sacrifice of the Cross sacramentally through the members of His Mystical Body and in particular through the ordained priest at the altar.

I believe there is no greater act of love, reparation and adoration than the Sacrifice of the Mass. We adore You Christ and we bless You, because by the holy Cross You have redeemed the world.* Amen.

Holy Eucharist: Blessesd Sacrament

Lord Jesus, I believe that You are truly present in Your Body, Blood, Soul and Divinity under the appearances of bread and wine in the Most Blessed Sacrament of the Altar contained in the tabernacles of our Catholic Church. "O Sacrament most holy, O Sacrament divine, all praise and all thanksgiving be every moment Thine."**

I adore You O Christ Who are truly present in this most

---

*From the Stations of the Cross
**From the Benediction hymn "O Sacrament Most Holy"

august Sacrament. You have promised to remain with us always. You are always present for our adoration and to receive our love and give us love in return, in our tabernacles. I turn my thoughts and my heart to You, Lord Jesus, as You dwell as the hidden Jesus under the veil of sacramental forms. You are as truly present as You were when You taught the Apostles in Palestine, when You became transfigured on Mt. Tabor with Your face shining bright as the sun and Your clothes as white as newly fallen snow under the glistening sun-light. You are the same Jesus Who once hung upon the Cross, only now in this most holy Sacrament, You are present as the glorified and risen Christ.

Accept my faith. I believe Lord, help my unbelief (Mk. 9:24). Purify my every intention with the love Your own sweet Mother had for Your adorable Heart. I offer Your Real Presence to the Most Holy Trinity in reparatory love for my own past sins and those of the world. Look not upon my weaknesses, O heavenly Father, but see only the infinitely pure love of the Eucharistic Heart of Your Son Jesus Christ present in the Blessed Sacrament. I unite myself with Him and together with His perfect offering of self in union with all the members of His Mystical Body, I join the offering of myself unto the glory of the Most Holy and Blessed Trinity. Amen.

Devotions before Holy Communion

Prayer of St. Thomas Aquinas:

Almighty and eternal God, behold I approach the Sacrament of Your only begotten Son, our Lord Jesus Christ. I approach as one who is sick to the physician of life, as one unclean to the fountain of mercy, as one blind to the light of eternal brightness, as one poor and needy to the Lord of heaven and earth. Therefore I beseech You, of Your infinite goodness, to heal my sickness, to wash away my filth, to enlighten my blindness, to enrich my poverty, and to clothe my nakedness, that I may receive the Bread of angels, the King of kings, and the Lord of lords with such reverence and humility, with such contrition and devotion, with such purity and faith, with such purpose and intention, as may conduce to the salvation of my soul. Grant, I beseech You, that I may receive not only the Sacrament of the body and Blood of our Lord, but also the fruit and virtue of this Sacrament. O most indulgent God, grant me so to receive the body of Your only-begotten Son, our Lord Jesus Christ, which He took of the Virgin Mary, that I may be found worthy to be incorporated with His mystical body and numbered among His members. O most loving Father, grant that I may one day contemplate forever, face to face, Your beloved Son, whom now on my pilgrimage I am about to receive, under the sacramental veils; who lives and reigns with You in the unity of the Holy Spirit, God, world without end. Amen.

Prayer of St. Ambrose:

O loving Lord Jesus Christ, I a sinner, presuming not on my own merits, but trusting in Your mercy and goodness, with fear and trembling approach the table of Your most sacred banquet. For I have defiled both my heart and body with many sins, and have not kept a strict guard over my mind and my tongue. Wherefore, O gracious God, O awful Majesty, I, a wretched creature, entangled in difficulties, have recourse to You the fount of mercy; to You do I fly that I may be healed, and take refuge under Your protection, and I ardently desire to have Him as my Savior, whom I am unable to withstand as my Judge. To You, O Lord, I show my wounds; to You I lay bare my shame. I know that my sins are many and great, on account of which I am filled with fear. But I trust in Your mercy, of which there is no end. Look down upon me, therefore, with the eyes of Your mercy, O Lord Jesus Christ, eternal King, God and Man, crucified for me. Hearken unto me, for my hope is in You; have mercy on me who am full of misery and sin, You who will never cease to let flow the fountain of mercy. Hail, Victim of salvation, offered for me and for all mankind on the tree of the cross. Hail, noble and precious Blood, flowing from the wounds of my crucified Lord Jesus Christ and washing away the sins of the whole world.

Remember, O Lord, Your creature, whom You have redeemed with Your Blood. I am grieved because I have sinned; I desire to make amends for what I have done. Take away from me, therefore, O most merciful Father, all my iniquities and sins, that, being purified both in soul and body, I may worthily partake of the holy of holies; and grant that this holy oblation of

Your Body and Blood, of which though unworthy I propose to partake, may be to me the remission of my sins, the perfect cleansing of my offenses, the means of driving away all evil thoughts and of renewing all holy desires, the accomplishment of works pleasing to You, as well as the strongest defense for soul and body against the snares of my enemies. Amen.

(By Fr. Fox):

"O Lord, I am not worthy that You should come under my roof; only say the word and my soul shall be healed"(Mt 8:8, and the Mass). Lord Jesus Christ, I desire to be united to You, to receive Your precious Body and Blood, together with Your Soul and Divinity. You are my Lord and my God and now, unworthy though I am, You are willing to come into my poor and sinful soul. I believe that I am at least in the state of grace, with all my many weaknesses. I am in grace, through no merits of my own, but only because of Your Divine mercy and forgiveness. I desire that You flood my soul more abundantly with your Divine life, with sanctifying grace, as You come into my body and soul.

O Jesus Mercy, I give You my heart and my soul. Take all I am and all that I have, O most loving Jesus, through Mary Your holy Mother. I desire to receive You in purity of heart and never be separated from You again. I thank You for this magnificent privilege which is possible only through Your merciful love. Amen.

Devotions After Holy Communion

ADORATION: My Lord and my God, Jesus Christ, You are truly living and substantially present within me with Your sacred Body, precious Blood, Your Soul and Divinity. I adore You profoundly. I rejoice in the union with Your all pure and holy humanity which is in heaven, in the Holy Eucharist and now within me as in a tabernacle. As you eternally praise and adore the Most Blessed Trinity in Your humanity as Mediator between heaven and earth, so now, within me, O Divine Priest, give infinite glory to God the Father, to the Word and to the Holy Spirit according as their infinite Divine Majesty deserves, in boundless measure. In union with You, Jesus Christ, my Lord, my God, my brother,I bow in adoration before the Most Blessed Trinity, declaring my nothingness, surrendering my entire self and being unto the eternal embrace of the Divine Will.

LOVE: Lord Jesus, true God and true man, present now within my body and soul, I ask You to take every faculty of my soul to know and love the Most Blessed Trinity, Father, Son and Holy Spirit. As You surrendered to the Father in the unity of the Holy Spirit of Love, I now, in union with the love of Your Sacred Heart, desire to give all that I am and all that I have unto the Holy Three in One. I desire that no impure affection of my body or soul shall ever taint Your grace within me.

THANKSGIVING: Lord God, my Savior, You have given me All, Your very Self, and so often I have replied only with ingratitude. But now, having You, Lord Jesus Christ, within my heart, I ask of Your Eucharistic and Sacred Heart to render to the Most Holy Trinity Your own infinite thanksgiving on my behalf and that of the world. I am all Yours and all that I have is Yours. I thank You for faith, for love, for grace, for coming into my soul so intimately.

REPARATION: Lord Jesus, may Your coming into me now make reparation to the Divine justice so often offended by the sins of humanity, including my own. As the Sacrifice of the Mass perpetuates the Sacrifice of the cross, so now may my union with You meritoriously gain the removal of the temporal punishment due to my past sins. May this Communion obtain deliverance of souls from purgatory and unite me more perfectly to You the Divine Victim on the Altar of the Cross. May I die to self and live to You.

PETITION: Lord Jesus, Your Divine Word reveals that in heaven You live constantly making intercession for us upon earth. That same intercession with God the Father through Your Sacred Humanity, in the unity of the Holy Spirit, You make in the Holy Eucharist, and in Your sacramental Presence now within me. I join my humble petitions to the infinitely pleasing petitions You now make within me as I pray especially for (name request).

Amen.

The Anima Christi of St. Ignatius Loyola

Soul of Christ, sanctify me.
Body of Christ, save me.
Blood of Christ, inebriate me.
Water from the side of Christ, wash me.
Passion of Christ, strengthen me.

O good Jesus, hear me.
Within Your wounds hide me.
Suffer me not to be separated from You.
From the malicious enemy defend me.
In the hour of my death call me.
And bid me come unto You.
That with Your saints I may praise You.
For ever and ever. Amen.

Part V
THE CHURCH

Church Militant, Church Persecuted

Peace and Freedom of All Peoples

Church Suffering: Purgatory

Church Triumphant: Saints

To St. Joseph for the Church

To a Patron Saint

Dedication to One's Guardian Angel

All Holy Angels

Church Militant, Church Persecuted

O Divine Head of the Mystical Body, Jesus Christ, look upon Your holy Church upon earth, in so many places suffering attacks within and without. Grant freedom unto Your Church, Divine Lord, for it is Your Body and You live within its members.

O Holy Spirit, Soul of the Mystical Body, grant wisdom to our Holy Father the Pope, and to the bishops whom we pray may be kept closely united under the chief Vicar of Jesus Christ upon earth. Sanctify the members of holy Church and keep them faithful in Divine love.

Heavenly Father, forgive the persecutors of the Church, bring them to conversion from their sins and win for the Church courage and unity so that it may be instrumental in the salvation of souls unto Your Divine glory. Amen.

Peace and Freedom of Peoples

Lord Jesus, Prince of Peace, grant freedom to all peoples of the world, especially those experiencing suppression of human rights and of the dignity that You intend the children of God to enjoy upon earth.

In union with the Immaculate Heart of Mary, the Queen of Peace, I implore Your Divine Majesty to grant deliverence to all peoples of the earth from all forms of slavery and especially grant peace and freedom to those living under atheistic Communism.

I offer to the Most Holy Trinity, the Body, Blood, Soul and Divinity of Jesus Christ being offered at Holy Mass at this moment throughout the world for the conversion of Russia and in reparation for all governments that suppress the rights of peoples.

Grant us, O Lord, that peace which the world cannot give (Jn. 14:27). Amen.

Church Suffering: Purgatory

O Lady of heaven, sweet Mother of God, with Your Divine Son and the Angels of which You are Queen, descend into purgatory and release souls from the fires of mercy and Divine justice. While the souls suffer in justice, it is by the mercy of God that, even though they are imperfect upon leaving this world, they are permitted a time of purgation after the death of their bodies so that they may become undefiled and enter into everlasting glory.

It is a holy and wholesome thought to pray for the dead, as Your Divine Word has revealed, Almighty God (2Mc. 12:43-46). I offer the precious Blood of Jesus present at this moment in all the chalices of the world where the Sacrifice of the Mass is being offered in reparation for the temporal punishment still due to the suffering souls in purgatory. Accept the infinite Sacrifice of Your Son being perpetuated on our altars througout the world.

O Saints of heaven, pray for the souls in purgatory that they may soon enter into glory with You. Unite your prayers to mine as I offer my prayers, works, joys and sufferings of this day, for I live yet in the time of merit, now deprived the souls in purgatory.

O Queen of the Angels, grant to the souls who are not yet ready and worthy of heavenly glory, relief from some of their miseries, and speed the day of their deliverance.

Eternal rest grant unto them, O Lord; and let perpetual light shine upon them. May the souls of all the faithful departed, through the mercy of God, rest in peace.* Amen.

Church Triumphant: Saints

O Saints of God, You who live before the heavenly Throne of the Most Blessed Trinity, take our acts of petition, thanksgiving, adoration and reparation to Almighty God. Lay our poor humble lives before the Divine Majesty.

Approach the Most Blessed Trinity through the Sacred Heart of Jesus, in union with Mary the Mother of God, St. Joseph, and my Guardian Angel, and pray for us your weak and sinful brothers and sisters still upon earth. Remind Almighty God, that, just as His Divine Son once died for our sins and weaknesses upon earth, so now He may permit our sins and faults to be purified in the most precious blood of Jesus Christ.

Ask the heavenly Father to gaze upon the glorified and sacred

---

*From the Mass for the Dead.

wounds in the hands and feet of Jesus Christ and look into the glorified pierced side of our loving Savior, and send forth from those five most precious wounds abundant graces to save us from our sins and bring us to the glory of heaven. Amen.

To St. Joseph for the Church

St. Joseph, virginal father of Jesus Christ, husband of Mary, Mother of God, to You do I come pleading for your intercession that I may always be pure in heart, unattached to this world, just in all the Christian virtues, and ever close to the Sacred Heart of Jesus and to the Immaculate Heart of Mary.

Grant me a profound faith and spirit of obedience such as you knew and manifested upon earth. Protect holy Church today as once You protected the Holy Family. Keep the Church always faithful and loyal to Jesus Christ under the loving mantle of Your spouse, sweet Mother Mary.

As you represented God the Father to Jesus Christ, so be to us a loving father and by your example and prayers of intercession form us in faith, love and obedience in your virginal Son, Jesus Christ.

O Joseph most just, pray for holy Church upon earth. Amen.

To a Patron Saint

O_____ (name saint), saint of heaven whose name I bear upon earth, intercede for me with the Most Blessed Trinity through the Sacred Heart of Jesus, the Mediator between heaven and earth.

Obtain for me an increase of faith, hope and charity. Help me to live all the Christian virtues in greater perfection and come to appreciate the living of the beatitudes as the fulfillment of the true Christian life upon earth which strengthens the Church and leads to heavenly glory. Amen.

Dedication to One's Guardian Angel[*]

HOLY, HOLY, HOLY LORD GOD OF HOSTS, HEAVEN AND EARTH ARE FULL OF YOUR GLORY (Rv. 4:8, and the Mass).

Kneeling before Your Majesty, we thank You, O God that You have given each of us a heavenly companion to be at our side, one who leads us according to Your will, directs us in Your paths and manifests to us Your love.

We resolve here in Your presence to love our holy companion as a brother, and to obey him when he speaks to us through

---

[*] According to the international movement in honor of the Angels, **Opus Sanctorum Angelorum.**

the voice of conscience. He will surely lead us to heaven.

Lord Jesus Christ, our Savior, take my hand and place it in the hand of my Guardian Angel and make the sign of our Redemption over it, Your blessing, for our salvation. In the name of the Father, and of the Son and of the Holy Spirit. Amen.

So speaks the Lord God: "I send my Angel before you to guard you as you go and to bring you to the place that I have prepared. Give him reverence and listen to all that he says. Offer him no defiance; he would not pardon such a fault, for my Name is in him"(Ex. 23:20).

All Holy Angels

Holy Angels of God, You who behold always the face of our Father in heaven, assist me in proclaiming the majesty, holiness, love and justice of God. May I unite with all you holy Angels in view of the disturbing times when the fallen angels labor to gain control over the world.

You holy Angels, messengers of God, spiritual beings without bodies, you are warriors who challenge men's mediocrity in the battle for the honor and glory of the Most Blessed Trinity and the salvation of souls.

Holy Angels of God, lead me to deeper faith in the existence of God, Three in One. Lead me to faith in and love for Jesus Christ, the Word made flesh, and for His Holy Catholic Church. Lead me to venerate Mary, the Mother of God, who is Your Queen as well as the Queen of men.

Holy Angels, You are filled with awe at the Incarnation, the Word made flesh, and you long to contemplate this great Mystery before the Most Blessed Sacrament. Come with me whenever I come before the Real Presence of our Eucharistic King and there with me adore the Divine Presence in the Word made flesh.

Unite with me, Holy Angels of God, in all that I do, my daily works, joys, prayers and sufferings. Keep me pure through your intercession and pray with me always. Amen.

Part VI
THE LAST THINGS

For a Happy Death

Act of Resignation

Judgement

Heaven: True Home

Rosary Decade Prayer

In Grief

Indulgences

Sacrifice Prayer

For a Happy Death*

Jesus, Mary and Joseph, I give you my heart and soul.

Jesus, Mary and Joseph, assist me in my last agony.

Jesus, Mary and Joseph, let me breathe forth my spirit in peace with you.

From a sudden and unprovided death, deliver us, O Lord.

Act of Resignation of Pius X

O Lord, my God, from this moment do I accept from Your hands, with a quiet and trusting heart, whatsoever death You shall choose to send me, with its pains and griefs.

Judgement

Lord Jesus, assist me by your saving graces to live each day as though it were my last. Help me to remember my last end so that I will not sin.

O most kind God, Father of mercies and God of all consolation, it is your Divine will that no one who believes and hopes in you should perish. In your infinite mercy, look upon my poor

---

*From the **Enchiridion of Indulgences**, 1968.

soul and because of the passion and death of Your only Son, when I leave this world, grant me a merciful judgement.

Grant me the grace, Divine Lord, of final perseverance, that cleansed from every stain of sin by the most precious blood of Jesus Christ, I may enter into the everlasting life of eternal glory and live forever with all the angels and saints in the beatific vision of heaven. Amen.

Heaven: True Home

My loving Father, I believe that heaven is my true home. You have made me for Yourself and I shall find no rest until I rest in You.*

In heaven I shall behold the Most Blessed Trinity in what is called the beatific vision. I shall see God face to face, even as He is. All the infinite beauty of God shall shine before me in the splendor of heavenly glory. Your Divine word has revealed that eye has not seen, nor ear heard, nor has it even entered into the mind of man, what things God has prepared for those who love Him (1Cor. 2:9).

I am but on pilgrimage here below, dear God. The sufferings and trials of this life are temporary and not worthy to be compared with the eternal life of happiness which is to come. When I live in grace with the Most Blessed Trinity dwelling in

---

*St. Augustine.

my soul, I have already found my heaven upon earth, for heaven is where God is, and God is in my soul.

I long, eternal Trinity, for the time when I can rest in eternal peace and no longer behold You as through a glass darkly, but shall gaze upon You in infinite beauty, clearly visible, and the freshness of that first moment of loving embrace shall ever remain in heavenly bliss that knows no end (1Cor. 13:11-12). Amen.

Rosary Decade Prayer*

"O my Jesus, forgive us our sins, save us from the fires of hell, and lead all souls to heaven, especially those most in need of Your mercy."

In Grief

God of life and death, You have taken a beloved one from me. My heart is very heavy. I recall that Your Son, Jesus Christ, became man in all things except sin and that He groaned in sorrow at the death of His friend, Lazarus. I unite my grief with

---

*To be said after each decade of the Rosary, from prayers given to the Fatima children, approved by the Vatican.

Yours dear Jesus as You stood at the tomb of Lazarus.

O Virgin Mother, you know what it was like losing Your husband Joseph and then your Child, dying suspended between earth and heaven, with a sword piercing your sweet soul. To you do I come in sorrow, begging strength from your intercession, from you who fully understand what it is like to lose one so dear and close.

Share with me, dear Mother of God, the courage, the strong faith that you had in the future resurrection. Even after Jesus came back to life and ascended into heaven, you knew you were to be left alone for many years before your own assumption into heaven. You comforted the Apostles as their Queen and Mother during those years. Grant comfort to me now as I sorrow in pain at the loss by the separation that has come as a result of the sin of our first parents and my own sins. Wipe away my tears with the merciful love of your Immaculate Heart as you unite me with my loved one through the grace of the Sacred Heart of your Son Jesus Christ. Amen.

Indulgences

I humbly request of You, my Lord and my God, in virtue of the merits of my Lord Jesus Christ, that You grant me all the indulgences attached to my prayers and works of this day. I desire to enter into the dispositions necessary to gain whatever indulgences the Church grants for my works and prayers of this day, that I may satisfy Divine justice and assist the souls in purgatory. Amen.

Sacrifice Prayer*

"O my Jesus, it is for love of You, in reparation for the offenses committed against the Immaculate Heart of Mary, and for the conversion of poor sinners."

---

*To be said when offering something up to God, from prayers given to the Fatima children, approved by the Vatican.

Part VII
JESUS, SAVIOR

The Knowledge of Jesus

The Cross

Merciful Heart of Jesus

Consecration to the Sacred Heart of Jesus

Reparation to the Sacred Heart of Jesus

The Knowledge of Jesus

Divine Jesus, at Your conception when the Angel Gabriel announced that your Mother would conceive and bear a child to be called "Son of the Most High", the Virgin Mary inquired, "How can this be since I do not know man?" The Angel replied: "The Holy Spirit will come upon you and the power of the Most High will overshadow you; hence, the holy offspring to be born will be called Son of God." Twice your Mother was told Who her child would be: "the Son of God."

When Your Sweet Mother, the Mother of holy Love, visited her cousin Elizabeth, Elizabeth was filled with the Holy Spirit and cried out in a loud voice: "Blest are you among women and blest is the fruit of your womb. But who am I that the mother of my Lord should come to me?"

When you were born the Angel announced to the shepherds: "This day in David's city a savior has been born to you, the Messiah and Lord." When you were twelve years old you said to Mary and Joseph: "Why did you search for me? Did you not know I had to be in my Father's house?" You identified God as Your Father already at the age of twelve. When You were baptized in the river Jordan the voice of the Father was heard from heaven, "You are my beloved Son." And to the Apostle Philip You said, "He who sees me sees the Father also."

Protect us, dear Jesus, from the temptation to follow those who claim that You, the Word of God made flesh, did not know Who You were until after the Resurrection, thereby calling into question Your Divinity and your saving power. As One most perfectly in union with the Divine Will of the Father, from Whom

You had received everything that He is, in the unity of the Holy Spirit, You knew Your identity as Jesus Christ, Son of God, Savior. Surely Your Mother knew Who You were. As the best and holiest of mothers she related to You the identity of Your true Father in heaven from Your earliest days. Surely Joseph most just would not permit You to be decieved that he, rather than the Father, was Your natural father.

Jesus Christ, You are Lord, my Savior and I profess and accept You as my personal Savior, true God and true man, from this moment and always. Amen.

The Cross

Lord, as You took up Your Cross You knew that You must suffer for the redemption of the world. You said, "And I, if I be lifted up from the earth, will draw all things to me"(Luke 12:32).

It is one of the mysteries of faith, dear Lord, that although You had the Beatific Vision even from the womb of Mary, yet Your soul became sorrowful even unto death. You always knew clearly Who you were, Lord, as You prayed before Your death: "Father, I will that where I am, they also whom You have given me may be with me; in order that they may behold my glory, which You have given me, because you have loved me before the creation of the world. Just Father, the world has not known You, but I have known You, and these have known that You have sent me. . ."(John 19).

Lord, help me to be worthy of You in taking up my cross, for you said that unless I am willing to deny myself and take up my cross daily and follow You, I am not worthy of You (Lk. 9:23). Help me to take up my cross with courage and never become so discouraged as to throw aside the Cross. Let me not listen to the temptations of the enemy but let me remember that in carrying the Cross I can help others too by acts of reparation.

Dear Lord Jesus, may I remember that the closer you draw me to Yourself, the more I will experience the Cross. Yet You have promised "my yoke is sweet and my burden is light" (Mt. 11:30).

The Angels of God have never known the mercy of God, only His justice. And yet, as they see the Sign of the Cross in us, dear Lord, they discover the beauty of the Father's mercy and glory therein. May the Angels, especially my Guardian Angel, lead me to cherish the mercy of God to be found in the Cross.

While to the world the Cross means folly, stupidity and shame, yet to You, dear Lord, and to those with faith and love, it is wisdom that leads to glory. When I am despised for carrying the Cross, I will look to You dear Lord and see in the Cross the emblem of truth. Amen.

Merciful Heart of Jesus

O Sacred Heart of Jesus, pierced by a lance, whereby blood and water flowed out for the redemption of the world, I come to You begging for the grace of salvation and forgiveness of all my offenses and those of the whole world.

I am Yours and Yours I wish to be. May the beatings of Your most Sacred Heart tell unto God the Father in the unity of the Holy Spirit, that we Your brothers and sisters still upon earth, are united to You by faith and that we desire to be one with You through grace.

I wish to return to Your most Sacred Heart love for the love which You have for us. You so loved the world that you lay down Your life for our salvation in obedience unto death, even death on the Cross (Ph. 2:8).

O open side of Jesus, pierced by a lance, ocean of mercy, place me firmly into Your side, into Your most Sacred Heart, cleansing me in Your most precious blood so that in the sight of my heavenly Father, indwelt by the Holy Spirit, I may forever remain secure in the refuge of Your tender, loving and Sacred Heart. Amen.

Consecration to the Sacred Heart

O Sacred Heart of Jesus, filled with an ocean of infinite love, broken by the ingratitude of sinful mankind and pierced by my sins and those of the world, yet loving me and the world still, accept this my act of consecration unto Your most Sacred Heart. I am all Yours and all that I have is Yours, O most Sacred Heart of Jesus, through Mary Your holy Mother.

Take every faculty of my soul and body. Take all that I am

and all that I have. Draw me day by day, nearer and dearer to You.

Sacred Heart of Jesus, once in agony in the garden and upon the Cross, take pity on me and all who are separated from Your love. Grant grace unto the dying, especially those not now in grace, that they may yet come to salvation. May You still be recognized as Savior by those who live in the darkness of unbelief. Draw all mankind into the light of Your kingdom.

Bring back the cold and the indifferent. Lift up the fallen. Touch hardened hearts. Make fervent the lukewarm. Make zealous the fervent. O Jesus Christ, O Heart all burning with love for me and for everyone throughout the world, I freely consecrate myself and all of us today to Your most loving Heart. Never forsake us. Bring converts to Your One, Holy, Catholic and Apostolic Church. Instill the fire of Your Divine love in all of us. Amen.

Reparation to the Sacred Heart*

O Sacred Heart of Jesus, Your loving Heart is subjected throughout the world to cruel indifference, injury and sacrilege. Mindful of my own failing to show You proper adoration and love, I come to You now to ask Your forgiveness for myself and for the sins of others.

---

*Based on the Encyclical Misserentissimus Redemptor of Pius XI, 1928

I seek to offer atonement for the sins of those straying from the path of salvation who refuse to follow You, their Shepherd and Leader, and who strike out against our chief Vicar on earth, our holy Father, the Pope. Many have renounced their baptismal vows and cast off the sweet yoke of Your law. Bring them back, dear Shepherd of our souls.

I desire to make amends for the many offenses against Christian modesty in unbecoming dress and behavior, for the foul seductions which ensnare the feet of innocent children and youth, and for the frequent violation of Sundays and holy days, and for the blasphemies uttered against You and Your saints.

I wish to make amends to Your most Sacred Heart for the insults to which Your chief Vicar on earth and Your priests are subjected, and for those who neglect or receive You in sacrilege in the very Sacrament of Your Divine love while not in the state of sanctifying grace. I wish to offer reparation for the public crimes of nations who resist the rights and the teaching authority of the Church which You have founded and for governments which permit the murders of innocent human beings by abortion, even before these children have seen the light of day.

I offer to Your eternal Father that Sacrifice Your Sacred Heart once made on the Cross as perpetuated on our altars today. I offer this act of atonement in union with Your ever-Virgin Mother as she stood beneath the Cross and I join my intention to those of all the Saints and the pious faithful throughout the world.

Henceforth, I shall live a life of uncompromising faith, in purity of conduct, in the observance of the precepts of the Gospel especially that of charity. I promise to influence others to the best of my ability not to offend You. Amen.

Part VIII
MARY, MOTHER OF GOD

Mary and the Blessed Trinity

Sons of the Immaculate Heart

Trust in the Immaculate Heart

Consecration to the Immaculate Heart

Reparation to the Immaculate Heart

Mother of Sweetness

Mother of Vocations

Mary, Mother of Priests

Lady of the Rosary

Jesus through Mary

Mother of Holy Love

Lady of the Beatitudes

Enrollment in the Brown Scapular

Mary and the Blessed Trinity

O most Holy Trinity, Father, Son and Holy Spirit, I adore You profoundly in thanksgiving for the Woman of faith and of love which you have given Your holy Church so as to be the Mother of each one of us.

O Mother of the Church, assist me in offering all that I am and all that I have to the glory of the most Holy Trinity.

O Daughter of God the Father, intercede that I may always live in grace, sharing in the Divine life as a member of the Mystical Body of Christ.

O Spouse of the Holy Spirit, You who were overshadowed by the Third Person of the Holy Trinity, pray that my spirit may always be open to receive the Holy Spirit into the temple of my body so that, indwelt by this sweet Guest of my soul, I may always recognize You as my Mother and the Holy Trinity as my God.

When the veil of faith folds back, may I behold the Most Blessed Trinity face to face and You my Mother standing next to Jesus as both of You have made constant intercession for me upon earth unto the glory of the Three in One.

Amen

Sons of the Immaculate Heart

O Mary, You who conceived the Word of God in Your Immaculate Heart before You did in Your womb, grant unto our Holy Church Sons of your Immaculate Heart who will teach the Word of God faithfully, fully, lovingly, patiently, perseveringly, in season and out of season.

O Mary, Spouse of the Holy Spirit and Mother of the Church, grant unto your Sons the gift of living in faith and love as you did upon earth.

Your Divine Son, O Mary, said to His brothers and disciples, "He who hears you, hears me. He who rejects you, rejects me. And he who rejects me, rejects him who sent me"(Lk. 10:16). The voice of the Catholic Church, we sincerely believe, is the voice of Jesus Christ, the invisible Head of the Church.

Keep, O Immaculate Mother, your sons loyally united in faith and morals to the supreme teaching authority of the Pope who teaches and governs unto the sanctification of souls for the honor and glory of the Most Holy Trinity.

O Jesus Christ, eternal Word of God Incarnate, keep the Sons of Your Mother's Immaculate Heart in oneness of purpose, working daily for the upbuilding of Your Mystical Body upon earth.

Mary Immaculate, interceding with the Father, through Jesus Christ, sanctify your sons in truth, in the spirit of obedience, humility, faith, hope and charity, together with all the Christian virtues that form them into the likeness of Jesus Christ.

Gather the Sons of Your Heart, O Mary, around our Eucharistic Lord, present in His Body, Blood, Soul and Divinity. Develop in them a love for the Divine Liturgy, which perpetuates the Sacrifice of the Cross and unites them to their Resurrected Lord. As we were first given to you as Sons under the Cross of Calvary, may we always recognize ourselves as your Sons, O Mother of the Holy Eucharist, as we gather at Mass and before the Real Presence of Jesus Christ in the Most Blessed Sacrament.

Grant unto us a love, not only for your Son, Jesus Christ, but for all the members of His Mystical Body whom we shall serve and teach unto the sanctification of their souls. Amen.

Trust in the Immaculate Heart

To the refuge of your Immaculate Heart, O heavenly Mother Mary, I come to be enclosed as in a most choice garden of sweetness and delight. I am the (son/daughter) of your Immaculate Heart, O Mother of God. You, O Spouse of the Holy Spirit, Daughter of God the Father, Mother of the Son, in your loving intimate relationship to the Most Blessed Trinity, serve as Mediatrix of all grace that comes to me from the heavenly throne, flowing forth from the Sacred Heart of Your Son, passing through the Immaculate Heart of your heavenly intercession.

The love of your Immaculate Heart showing forth in tender care gives me confidence in You, O heavenly Mother Mary. In you I trust. Your intercession, united to the Sacred Heart of Jesus, is powerful to tend to every need of body and soul upon earth and to lead me lovingly home to your eternal embrace, where you will introduce me to your Divine Son and to the entire Blessed Trinity.

My Mother, my Confidence, be to me always the Intercessor who anticipates the very graces I ask for and those I forget to seek. Keep me always united to your Son, with the Holy Spirit dwelling always in my soul, and the heavenly Father forever providing for my every temporal and spiritual need as all three Persons in the one Godhead see in you, O Mary, the Mother of this your (son/daughter) upon earth. Amen.

Consecration to the Immaculate Heart

Heavenly Mother Mary, I come to your most loveable and sweet Heart, refuge of sinners. I offer myself to you and consecrate my entire life to your Immaculate Heart. In this consecration of my total person, I offer you my body and soul with all its miseries and weaknesses. I offer you my heart with all its affections and desires, my prayers, works, joys and sufferings. I offer you every temptation that comes to me so that my every thought and desire may be purified through your holy intercession.

My Queen, my Mother, I offer you in consecration all sufferings which come into my life, both physical and spiritual. I offer you especially my death with all that will accompany it. I offer you my last agony. Accept all this, my Mother, and take all into your Immaculate Heart as I give to you irrevocably all that I am and all that I have, together with all property and possessions. I offer you my family and all who are near and dear to me. Take them all into your Immaculate Heart and keep us ever one in your Son Jesus Christ.

I renew today the vows of my Baptism and Confirmation. Keep me ever faithful to God and to Holy Church, and loyal in obedience to the Holy Father, the Pope. I desire to pray the Rosary properly, meditating on its mysteries. I desire to participate in the Sacrifice of your Son perpetuated at Holy Mass and receive Him frequently, even daily, in Holy Communion. I attach special importance to the first Saturday of the month in reparation to your Immaculate Heart and I will work for the conversion of sinners. I will strive to live daily the spirit of Eucharistic reparation.

O Queen of the Angels, my Queen and my Mother, I humbly prostrate myself before you as I approach you with my Guardian Angel. I desire all the holy angels, and especially my Guardian, to venerate you always as Queen of heaven and earth. Command my Guardian and all holy angels to keep me always in your love and in the union of grace with your Divine Son. Send forth your angels to assit me in spreading devotion to your Immaculate Heart so that through your intercession there may be peace in the world and in the Church, and the Kingdom of Christ may come on earth as it is in heaven. Amen.

Reparation to the Immaculate Heart

Immaculate Mother, I come to you to offer my love, my very life, and my Confession and Holy Communion in reparation for the sins committed against your all holy and Immaculate Heart. I desire too to offer the holy Rosary and meditation on its mysteries in reparation to your Immaculate Heart.

I offer these acts in reparation to you, O Mary Immaculate,

especially for the following reasons:

- In reparation for the blasphemies that are uttered against your Immaculate Conception;
- In reparation for those who deny your perpetual Virginity and speak in any way against your holiness;
- In reparation for those who deny your Divine Maternity, refusing at the same time to accept you as the Mother of all mankind;
- In reparation for those who try publicly to implant in the hearts of children indifference, contempt, and even hatred toward your Immaculate Heart;
- In reparation for those who insult you directly in your holy statues and images.

O Mother of God and Mother of men, Mother mine, take me as your child, grant comfort to my poor sinful heart, even as I desire to grant comfort and offer reparation to your Sorrowful and Immaculate Heart. Amen.*

Mother of Sweetness**

Mother of Sweetness, the faith and love with which you gave us your Divine Son urges me to open my heart to the love

---

*Recommended for First Saturday devotions along with confession, communion, and five decades of the Rosary with at least fifteen minutes of meditation.
**Inspired by a portrait of Our Lady by Bro. Gino Burresi, O.M.V.

of your heart so that the sweetness of your Mother's love may touch me deeply. May the sweetness of your heart cause me to share with others your love for Jesus.

As I meditate on the mysteries of Jesus Christ in the most holy Rosary, ever-Virgin Mother Mary, reveal to me the sweetness of your own Immaculate Heart. Amen.

Mother of Vocations

Pray, we beg you, O holy Mother of the Church, that young men answer the call of your Son Jesus Christ, "Come follow me." O Mother of Vocations, whisper to boys and young men to give their entire lives as Sons of your Immaculate Heart so that they may become other Christs. Grant them the vocations to become fathers of souls.

Pray, we beg you again, O Mother of Vocations, that girls and young ladies hear and answer the call of your Sweet Heart as you plead for your Son, Jesus Christ. Grant them courage to become mothers of souls in the consecrated religious life.

Keep the chosen souls of your Divine Son holy and pure, prayerful and faithful, so that they may always be living sacrifices for the honor and glory of God. Amen.

Mary, Mother of Priests

I pray, O heavenly ever-Virgin Mother of God, for all priests of holy Church that they may enter into the temple of your Immaculate Heart. Keep them pure and holy. Keep them under the mantle of your heavenly intercession and motherly protection. Keep them always loyal to your Son Jesus Christ and in union with their bishops united to the Pope.

Protect priests, "other Christs", from the onslaughts of Satan. As you once crushed the head of Satan by the fruit of your holy womb, so drive back the forces of hell that assail your Son in the persons of His ordained priests, whose precious souls bear the indelible character of your sole begotten Son made man, Who is also the only begotten of God the Father by the overshadowing of the Holy Spirit.

We live in a time when Satan wages war on the Church, the Mystical Body, as never before. The forces of evil strive hardest to destroy the beauty of Christ's image and character in the souls of priests, who are copies of Christ. Forgive me for the times I have been critical of these priests, O Mary, whose Queen and Mother you are. Grant me the wisdom to pray for priests rather than criticize them, for I need your priests to give me the Body, Blood, Soul and Divinity of your Son Jesus Christ in Holy Communion and to adore the Blessed Trinity through the perpetuation of the Sacrifice of the Cross which is the holy Mass.

Your priests are vessels of clay and yet possessed of the greatest dignity and power possible to man upon earth, the dignity and power of your only Son, the High Priest Jesus Christ. In the temple of your Heart, purify and strengthen your priests to preach the true Word of God in unity with the Magisterium, so that faith and love in Jesus Christ may reign upon the earth. Amen.

Lady of the Rosary

O heavenly Mother of God and our Mother too, we come to you who have manifested yourself as our Lady of the Rosary, to beg for peace in the world, peace in the Church and peace in our hearts.

Lady of the holy Rosary, you are the Mother of the Word, Mother of the mysteries of Christ. As we pray your holy Rosary, we beg you, pray with us, meditating on the mysteries of your Son, Jesus Christ.

We believe that you will obtain for us all that we ask through your holy Rosary, for the proper praying of the Rosary is contemplation of the chief joyful, sorrowful and glorious events in the life of your Son, Our Lord Jesus Christ, Who leads us to salvation through your intercession.

O Queen of the holy Rosary, obtain that peace which the world cannot give or obtain of itself. I believe that the peace of the world has been confided to the intercession of your Immaculate Heart and that through the praying of the Rosary your intercession is made efficacious unto the Blessed Trinity.

As we pray the Rosary and meditate upon the mysteries of Christ in union with You, O heavenly Virgin Mary, shed the light of your Immaculate Heart upon us that we too may penetrate the secrets of the King of heaven and earth. Amen.

Jesus Through Mary*

Mary the Dawn, Christ the Perfect Day;
Mary the gate, Christ the Heavenly Way!

Mary the root, Christ the Mystic Vine;
Mary the grape, Christ the Sacred Wine!

Mary the wheat, Christ the Living Bread;
Mary the stem, Christ the Rose blood-red!

Mary the font, Christ the Cleansing Flood;
Mary the cup, Christ the Saving Blood!

Mary the temple, Christ the temple's Lord;
Mary the shrine, Christ the God adored!

Mary the beacon, Christ the Haven's Rest;
Mary the mirror, Christ the Vision Blest!

Mary the mother, Christ the mother's Son,
By all things blest while endless ages run. Amen.

---

*From the hymn in the Common of the Blessed Virgin Mary, Liturgy of the Hours.

Mother of Holy Love*

Mary, Mother of Christ, Mother of holy Love, do you yourself form us according to the Heart of your Son.

Lady of the Beatitudes

Blest are you, O Virgin Mother of God,
Who surrendered your spirit entirely to the Lord;
  You now reign with God forever.

Blest are you who sorrowed upon earth from the conception to the death of your Son, Jesus Christ;
  Your Heart was pierced with a sword.
    You are now consoled forever and are a consolation to us.

Blest are you, O Heavenly Mother Mary.
  God regarded the humility of you His handmaid,
    And now you inherit heaven and earth and all creation.

Blest are you, O Virgin Mother, who hungered and thirsted with your Son to do the will of the Father.
  Full of grace upon earth,
    You now intercede for our holiness.

Blest are you, Mother of Mercy.
  You received the highest mercy in being conceived Immaculate.
    You now obtain for us Mercy from the Heart of your Son.

---

*By Abbot Marmion.

Blest are you, O Immaculate Heart of Mary,
> Who upon earth were single-hearted in believing and loving.
>> You now see God face to face and intercede to lead us to the same beatific vision.

Blest are you, Mother and Queen of Peace.
> You pray for peace in the Church and in the world;
>> You are the highly favored Daughter of God the Father,
>> And care for your sons and daughters still upon earth.

Blest are you, O Mother of Jesus Christ, who were persecuted for holiness' sake.
> What was done to Jesus was done to you, and men still treat you this way.
>> The reign of God is yours.

Enrollment in the Brown Scapular*

The person who is to receive the habit kneels and the priest, vested in surplice and white stole says:

V. Show us, O Lord, your mercy.
R. And grant us your salvation.
V. O Lord, hear my prayer.
R. And let my cry come to you.
V. The Lord be with you.
R. And with your spirit.

Let us pray. O Lord Jesus Christ, Savior of mankind, by your right hand sanctify this scapular which your servant will devoted-

---

*From the 1964 **English Ritual**.

ly wear for the love of you and of your Mother, the blessed Virgin Mary of Mount Carmel. By her intercession may he be protected from the wickedness of the enemy and persevere in Your grace until death, who live and reign for ever and ever.

R. Amen.

Then the priest sprinkles the scapular with holy water and imposes it upon the person (or upon each person), saying:

Receive the blessed scapular and ask the most holy Virgin that, by her merits, it may be worn with no stain of sin and may protect you from all harm and bring you into everlasting life.

R. Amen.

After this the priest adds:

By the power granted to me, I admit you to a share in all the spiritual works performed with the merciful help of Jesus Christ by the religious of Mount Carmel. In the name of the Father and of the Son and of the Holy Spirit.

R. Amen.

May almighty God, Creator of heaven and earth, bless you whom he has been pleased to receive into the Confraternity of the Blessed Virgin Mary of Mount Carmel. We beg her to crush the head of the ancient serpent in the hour of your death and to obtain for you the palm and the crown of your everlasting inheritance. Through Christ our Lord.

R. Amen.

The priest sprinkles the person with holy water. For several persons, the prayers are said in the plural. If the scapular is to be blessed alone, begin with **V.** Show us, O Lord your mercy, and conclude with 'O Lord Jesus Christ....'

Part IX
LITANIES*

Litany of the Sacred Heart of Jesus

Litany of the Immaculate Heart of Mary

Litany of St. Joseph

Litany of the Angel Guardian

Litany of the Saints

---

*From the **Enchiridion of Indulgences**, 1968, and other traditional sources, adapted by Fr. Fox.

Litany of the Sacred Heart of Jesus

Lord, have mercy on us.
Christ, have mercy on us.
Lord, have mercy on us.

Christ, hear us.
Christ, graciously hear us.

God the Father of heaven, have mercy on us.
God the Son, Redeemer of the world, have mercy on us.
God the Holy Spirit, have mercy on us.

Holy Trinity, one God, have mercy on us.

Heart of Jesus, Son of the Eternal Father, have mercy on us (etc.).
Heart of Jesus, formed in the womb of the Virgin Mother by the Holy Spirit,
Heart of Jesus, united substantially with the Word of God,
Heart of Jesus, holy temple of God,
Heart of Jesus, tabernacle of the Most High,
Heart of Jesus, house of God and gate of heaven,
Heart of Jesus, glowing furnace of charity,
Heart of Jesus, of infinite majesty,
Heart of Jesus, full of goodness and love,
Heart of Jesus, abyss of all virtues,
Heart of Jesus, most worthy of all praise,
Heart of Jesus, king and center of all hearts,
Heart of Jesus, in which are all the treasures of wisdom and knowledge,
Heart of Jesus, in which dwelleth all the fullness of Divinity,
Heart of Jesus, in which the Father was well pleased,
Heart of Jesus, of whose fullness we have all received,
Heart of Jesus, desire of the eternal hills,
Heart of Jesus, patient and rich in mercy,
Heart of Jesus, rich to all who invoke You,
Heart of Jesus, vessel of justice and love,
Heart of Jesus, font of life and holiness,

Heart of Jesus, propitiation for our sins,
Heart of Jesus, saturated with revilings,
Heart of Jesus, crushed for our iniquities,
Heart of Jesus, made obedient unto death,
Heart of Jesus, pierced with a lance,
Heart of Jesus, source of all consolation,
Heart of Jesus, our life and resurrection,
Heart of Jesus, our peace and reconciliation,
Heart of Jesus, victim for our sins,
Heart of Jesus, salvation of those who hope in You,
Heart of Jesus, delight of all the Saints,

Lamb of God, Who take away the sins of the world, spare us O Lord.
Lamb of God, Who take away the sins of the world, graciously hear us, O Lord.
Lamb of God, Who take away the sins of the world, have mercy on us.

V. Jesus meek and humble of heart,
R. Make our hearts like unto Yours.

Let Us Pray

Almighty and everlasting God, graciously regard the Heart of Your well-beloved Son and the acts of praise and satisfaction which He renders You on behalf of us sinners, and through their merit, grant forgiveness in the name of Your Son, Jesus Christ, Who lives and reigns with You in the unity of the Holy Spirit, world without end. Amen.

Litany of the Immaculate Heart of Mary

Lord, have mercy on us.
Christ, have mercy on us.
Lord, have mercy on us.
Christ, hear us.

Christ, graciously hear us.

God the Father of heaven, have mercy on us.
God, the Son, Redeemer of the World, have mercy on us.
God the Holy Spirit, have mercy on us.
Holy Trinity, one God, have mercy on us.

Immaculate Heart of Mary, favorite Daughter of God the Father, pray for us.
Immaculate Heart of Mary, Mother of God the Son, pray for us (etc.)
Immaculate Heart of Mary, Spouse of the Holy Spirit,
Immaculate Heart of Mary, redeemed in a sublime manner by the merits of your Son,
Immaculate Heart of Mary, Mother and Model of the church,
Immaculate Heart of Mary, excellent examplar in faith and charity,
Immaculate Heart of Mary, who conceived the Word of God in Your Heart before you did in your womb,
Immaculate Heart of Mary, Who gave precious Blood to the Son of God in His human nature,
Immaculate Heart of Mary, conceived free of Original Sin,
Immaculate Heart of Mary, who embraced God's saving will with a full heart, impeded by no sin,
Immaculate Heart of Mary, whose sweet soul a sword pierced beneath the Cross,
Immaculate Heart of Mary, given to us as Mother by Jesus as he hung dying on the Cross,
Immaculate Heart of Mary, who accepted us as sons as you stood beneath the Cross,
Immaculate Heart of Mary, all pure and holy,
Immaculate Heart of Mary, exalted by Divine grace above all angels and men,
Immaculate Heart of Mary, Mediatrix of all graces,

Lamb of God, who take away the sins of the world, spare us, O Lord!
Lamb of God, who take away the sins of the world, graciously hear us, O Lord!

Lamb of God, who take away the sins of the world, have mercy on us.

V. Pray for us, O holy Mother of God.
R. That we may be made worthy of the promises of Christ.

Let us pray.

O Immaculate Heart of Mary, beating with love for all your children upon earth, pray for us who have recourse to you. Show to our Heavenly Father the wound in the Heart of your Son and at the same time offer again the sword that pierced your sorrowful and Immaculate Heart as you suffered by compassion with your Divine Son for the redemption of the world. By your intercession, through the merits of Jesus Christ, bring us to salvation. Amen.

Litany of St. Joseph

Lord, have mercy.
Christ, have mercy.
Lord, have mercy.
Christ, hear us.
Christ, graciously hear us.
God, the Father of Heaven, have mercy on us.
God the Son, Redeemer of the world, have mercy on us.
God the Holy Spirit, have mercy on us.
Holy Mary, pray for us.
St. Joseph, pray for us (etc).
Renowned offspring of David,
Light of Patriarchs,
Spouse of the Mother of God,
Chaste guardian of the Virgin,
Foster father of the Son of God,
Diligent protector of Christ,
Head of the Holy Family,
Joseph most just,
Joseph most chaste,
Joseph most prudent,
Joseph most strong,
Joseph most obedient,
Joseph most faithful,
Mirror of patience,
Lover of poverty,
Model of artisans,
Glory of home life,
Guardian of virgins,
Pillar of families,
Solace of the wretched,
Hope of the sick
Patron of the dying,
Terror of demons,

Protector of Holy Church,

Lamb of God, who take away the sins of the world, spare us, O Lord!
Lamb of God, who take away the sins of the world, graciously hear us, O Lord!
Lamb of God, who take away the sins of the world, have mercy on us.

V. He made him the lord of his household.
R. And prince over all his possessions.

Let Us Pray

O God, in your ineffable providence you were pleased to choose Blessed Joseph to be the spouse of your most holy Mother; grant, we beg you, that we may be worthy to have him for our intercessor in heaven whom on earth we venerate as our Protector; You who live and reign forever and ever. Amen.

Litany of the Angel Guardian

Lord, have mercy on us!
Christ, have mercy on us!
Lord, have mercy on us!

Christ, hear us!
Christ, graciously hear us!

God the Father of Heaven, have mercy on us!
God the Son, Redeemer of Men, have mercy on us!
God the Holy Spirit, have mercy on us!

Holy Trinity, one God, have mercy on us.

Holy Mary, Queen of Heaven, pray for us!

Holy Angel, my Guardian, pray for us (etc.)
Holy Angel, my Protector in all dangers,
Holy Angel, my Defense in all afflictions,

Holy Angel, most faithful Lover,
Holy Angel, my Preceptor
Holy Angel, my Guide,
Holy Angel, Witness of all my actions,
Holy Angel, my Helper in all my difficulties,
Holy Angel, my Negotiator with God,
Holy Angel, my Advocate,
Holy Angel, lover of Chastity,
Holy Angel, lover of Innocence,
Holy Angel, most obedient to God,
Holy Angel, Director of my Soul.
Holy Angel, model of Purity,
Holy Angel, model of Docility,
Holy Angel, my Counsellor in doubt,
Holy Angel, my Guardian through life,
Holy Angel, my Shield at the hour of death,

Lamb of God, who take away the sins of the world, spare us, O Lord!
Lamb of God, who take away the sins of the world, hear us, O Lord!
Lamb of God, who take away the sins of the world, have mercy on us!

V. Be the Savior of your faithful people, Lord.
R. Grant them your blessing, for they belong to you.

Litany of the Saints

Lord, have mercy.
Christ, have mercy.
Lord, have mercy.
Christ, hear us.
Christ, graciously hear us.
God the Father of Heaven, have mercy on us.
God the Son, Redeemer of the world, have mercy on us.
God the Holy Spirit, have mercy on us.
Holy Trinity, one God, have mercy on us.
Holy Mary, pray for us, (etc).

Holy Mother of God,
Holy Virgin of virgins,
St. Michael,
St. Gabriel,
St. Raphael,
All you holy Angels and Archangels,
All you holy orders of blessed Spirits,
St. John the Baptist,
St. Joseph,
All you holy patriarchs and Prophets,
St. Peter,
St. Paul
St. Andrew,
St. James,
St. John,
St. Thomas,
St. Philip,
St. Bartholomew,
St. Matthew,
St. Simon,
St. Thaddeus,
St. Matthias,
St. Barnabas,
St. Luke,
St. Mark,
All you holy Apostles and Evangelists,
All you holy Disciples of the Lord,
All you holy Innocents,
St. Stephen,
St. Lawrence,
St. Vincent,
Sts. Fabian and Sebastian,
Sts. John and Paul,
Sts. Cosmas and Damian,
Sts. Gervase and Protase,
All you holy Martyrs,
St. Sylvester,
St. Gregory,
St. Ambrose,
St. Augustine,
St. Jerome,
St. Martin,
St. Nicholas,
All you holy Bishops and Confessors,
All you holy Doctors,
St. Anthony,
St. Benedict,
St. Bernard,
St. Dominic,
St. Francis,
All you holy Priests and Levites,
All you holy Monks and Hermits,
St. Mary Magdalen,
St. Agatha,
St. Lucy,
St. Agnes,
St. Cecilia,
St. Catherine,
St. Anastasia,
All you holy Virgins and Widows,
All you Holy Men and Women, Saints of God, make intercession for us.

Be merciful, spare us, O Lord.
Be merciful, graciously hear us, O

From all evil, O Lord, deliver us.
From all sin, O Lord, deliver us (etc).
From your wrath,
From sudden and unprovided death,
From the snares of the devil,
From anger, and hatred, and all ill-will,
From the spirit of fornication,
From lightning and tempest,
From the scourge of earthquake,
From plague, famine and war,
From everlasting death,
Through the mystery of your holy Incarnation,
Through your Coming,
Through your Nativity,
Through your Baptism and holy fasting,
Through your Cross and Passion,
Through your Death and Burial,
Through your holy Resurrection,
Through your admirable Ascension,
Through the coming of the Holy Spirit, the Paraclete,
In the day of judgment,
Lamb of God, who take away the sins of the world, spare us, O Lord.
Lamb of God, who take away the sins of the world, graciously hear us, O Lord.
Lamb of God, who take away the sins of the world, have mercy on us.
Christ, hear us.
Christ, graciously hear us.
Lord, have mercy.
Christ, have mercy.
Lord, have mercy.
Our Father, etc.
V. And lead us not into temptation.
R. But deliver us from evil.

Part X
THE ROSARY

How to Say the Rosary

Clause Method of Praying the Rosary

Meditation on the Holy Rosary

How to Say the Rosary

Those unfamiliar with the Rosary will find this brief explanation helpful. The Rosary consists of a circle of five large and fifty small beads, with the small beads separated by a large one after every ten beads, or decade. A short chain with a crucifix, one large bead and three small beads is attached to one of the large beads in the circle.

The Rosary begins on the Crucifix with the Apostles' Creed and proceeds up the short chain and then around the circle of beads. On the short chain: first large bead, Our Father; three small beads, Hail Mary on each bead (usually said for faith, hope and love); after third small bead but before the large bead which begins the circle, Glory Be to the Father. On the first large bead of the circle, Our Father; on the ten small beads following, Hail Mary on each; then the Glory Be in between beads, which brings up the next large bead. Continue the Our Father, ten Hail Mary, Glory Be sequence on each of the decades until back to the first large bead on the circle. After the last Glory Be, say the Hail Holy Queen. Make the sign of the Cross and, if desired, kiss the crucifix.

The Rosary is designed to occupy the lips, hands and mind in prayer. The key to its success is to meditate on the Glorious, Sorrowful or Joyful mysteries (see Meditation section), one for each decade.

The Rosary Decade Prayer (see Part Six) may be said after each Glory Be.

Clause Method of the Rosary

Pope Paul VI recommended the clause method, paragraph 46, **Marialis Cultus,** Feb. 2, 1974. One is to add to the name of Jesus in each Hail Mary a reference to the mystery being contemplated. This "clause" method has been mandated by the bishops of various European countries, e.g. Germany, Switzerland, Austria, Hungary, etc.

I. "Clauses" for the Joyful Mysteries:
   1...Jesus, whom thou hast conceived.
   2...Jesus, whom thou hast brought to St. Elizabeth.
   3...Jesus, who was born in Bethlehem.
   4...Jesus, whom thou hast offered in the temple.
   5...Jesus, whom thou hast found in the temple.

II. "Clauses" for the Sorrowful Mysteries:
   1...Jesus, who for us sweat blood.
   2...Jesus, who for us was scourged.
   3...Jesus, who for us was crowned with thorns.
   4...Jesus, who for us carried the heavy Cross.
   5...Jesus, who for us was crucified.

III. "Clauses" for the Glorious Mysteries:
   1...Jesus, who has risen from the dead
   2...Jesus, who has ascended into heaven.
   3...Jesus, who has sent the Holy Spirit.
   4...Jesus, who has taken you body and soul into heaven.
   5...Jesus, who has crowned you Queen of heaven and earth.

Meditation on the Holy Rosary

The proper praying of the holy Rosary requires meditation on one of the 15 mysteries of our faith for each decade. The various prayers of praise and petition make up the **body** of the Rosary. Meditation on the Joyful, Sorrowful or Glorious mysteries comprise the **soul** of the Rosary. The Joyful Mysteries are the Annunciation by Gabriel to our Lady, the Visitation of Mary to Elizabeth, the Nativity of Our Lord, the Presentation of the Child Jesus in the Temple, and the Finding of the Boy Jesus in the Temple; the Sorrowful Mysteries are the Agony of our Lord in the Garden, the Scourging at the Pillar, the Crowning with Thorns, the Carrying of the Cross, and the Crucifixion; the Glorious Mysteries are the Resurrection of our Lord, the Ascension of our Lord into Heaven, the Descent of the Holy Spirit at Pentecost, the Assumption of our Lady into Heaven, and the Coronation of our Lady as Queen of Heaven.

Pope Paul VI (**Marialis Cultus**) said: Without contemplation the "Rosary is a body without a soul, and its recitation is in danger of becoming a mechanical repetition. . . . By its nature the recitation of the Rosary calls for a quiet rhythm and a lingering pace, helping the individual to meditate on the mysteries of the Lord's life as seen through the eyes of her who was closest to the Lord. In this way the unfathomable riches of these mysteries are unfolded. . . .

"As a Gospel prayer, centered on the mystery of the redemptive Incarnation, the Rosary is therefore a prayer with a clearly Christological orientation."

In praying each decade it is well to request a particular Christian virtue which the meditation suggests. Below are two brief sample meditations, on the Crucifixion and the Resurrection; similar meditations can be devised for all the Joyful, Sorrowful and Glorious Mysteries.

THE CRUCIFIXION

"About the ninth hour Jesus cried out with a loud voice, saying . . . 'My God, my God, why have You forsaken me?'" (Mt. 27:46)

"Now there were standing by the cross of Jesus His Mother and His Mother's sister, Mary of Cleophas, and Mary Magdalene. When Jesus, therefore, saw His Mother and the disciple standing by, whom He loved, He said to His Mother, 'Woman, behold your son.' Then he said to the disciple, 'Behold your Mother.' And from that hour the disciple took her into his home." Then they gave him a sponge soaked in vinegar. Jesus tasted, then he said, "'It is consummated!' And bowing His head, He gave up His spirit" (Jn. 19:25-30).

I offer You Lord Jesus this decade in union with the mystery of Your crucifixion and death on the Cross, and ask of Your Mother's intercession, by the grace she merited in virtue of Your infinite merits flowing from the Cross, that (name at least one):

1) sinners might be converted; 2)I be ever mindful that holy Mass perpetuates the Sacrifice of the Cross; 3) I might recognize myself as a (son/daughter) of Mary as well as an adopted child of God.

THE RESURRECTION

Peter and John ran to the tomb when Mary Magdalene reported it empty on Easter Sunday morning. John got there first and waited for Peter. While waiting, John stooped down and saw the linen cloths lying there but did not enter. "Simon Peter therefore came following him, and he went into the tomb, and saw the linen cloths lying there. . . . Then the other disciple also went in. . . . And he saw and believed. . ."(John 20:3-9).

"When it was late that same day, the first of the week, though the doors where the disciples gathered had been closed . . . Jesus came and stood in their midst and said to them, 'Peace be to you' . . . He showed them His hands and His side. . . 'As the Father has sent me, I also send you.' When he had said this, he breathed upon them, and said to them, 'Receive the Holy Spirit; whose sins you shall forgive, they are forgiven them; and whose sins you shall retain, they are retained'" (John 20:19-23).

O Holy Mother, by the joy you experienced at the Resurrection and through the grace of this Mystery, obtain the grace (name at least one):

1) that I Have faith that I am a (son/daughter) of the Resurrection, destined to rise gloriously one day; 2) that all men everywhere may come to the fullness of true faith in Jesus Christ, Lord, God and Savior; 3) that all recognize that You Lord Jesus, having redeemed the world, gave to Your Church the power to forgive sins.

Part XI
PRAYERS LITTLE REMEMBERED

Apostles' Creed

Act of Faith

Act of Hope

Act of Love

Prayer to the Holy Spirit

Memorare

Prayer to St. Michael

The Apostles' Creed

I believe in God, the Father Almighty, Creator of heaven and earth; and in Jesus Christ, His only Son, our Lord; who was conceived by the Holy Spirit, born of the Virgin Mary, suffered under Pontius Pilate, was crucified, died and was buried. He descended into hell; the third day He arose again from the dead; He ascended into heaven, where he sits at the right hand of God, the Father Almighty; from thence He shall come to judge the living and the dead. I believe in the Holy Spirit, the Holy Catholic Church, the communion of saints, the forgiveness of sins the resurrection of the body, and life everlasting. Amen.

Act of Faith

O My God, I firmly believe that Thou art one God in three Divine Persons, Father, Son and Holy Spirit; I believe that Thy Divine Son became man and died for our sins, and that He will come to judge the living and the dead. I believe these and all the truths which the Holy Catholic Church teaches because Thou hast revealed them, Who canst neither deceive nor be deceived. Amen.

Act of Hope

O My God, relying on Thy almighty power and infinite mercy and promises, I hope to obtain pardon of my sins, the help of Thy grace, and life everlasting, through the merits of Jesus Christ, my Lord and Redeemer. Amen.

Act of Love

O My God, I love Thee above all things, with my whole heart and soul, because Thou art all good and worthy of all love. I love my neighbor as myself for the love of Thee. I forgive all who have injured me, and ask pardon of all whom I have injured. Amen.

Prayer to the Holy Spirit

Come Holy Spirit, fill the hearts of Thy faithful and kindle in them the fire of Thy love.
V. Send forth Thy Spirit, and they shall be created.
R. And Thou shalt renew the face of the earth.

Let us pray

O God, who didst instruct the hearts of the faithful by the light of the Holy Spirit, grant that, by the gift of the same Spirit, we may be always truly wise, and ever rejoice in His consolation. Through Jesus Christ our Lord. Amen.

The Memorare

Remember, O most gracious virgin Mary, that never was it known that anyone who fled to your protection, implored your help or sought your intercession was left unaided. Inspired with this confidence, I fly to you, O Virgin of virgins, my Mother. To you I come, before you I stand, sinful and sorrowful. O Mother of the Word Incarnate, do not ignore my petitions, but in your mercy hear and answer me. Amen.

Prayer to St. Michael

St. Michael the Archangel, defend us in battle; be our defense against the wickedness and snares of the devil. May God rebuke him, we humbly pray, and do you, O prince of the heavenly host, by the power of God, thrust into hell Satan and the other evil spirits who prowl about the world for the ruin of souls. Amen.